D1101598

GIN · VODKA · TEQUILA

GIN · VODKA · TEQUILA

150 CONTEMPORARY AND CLASSIC COCKTAILS

BRIAN LUCAS

DUNCAN BAIRD PUBLISHERS

LONDON

Gin · Vodka · Tequila
Brian Lucas

First published in the UK and USA in 2013
by Duncan Baird Publishers,
an imprint of Watkins Publishing Limited
Sixth Floor, 75 Wells Street
London W1T 3QH

A member of Osprey Group

Osprey Publishing Inc.
43-01 21st Street
Suite 220B, Long Island City
New York 11101

Managing Editor: Sarah Epton
Editors: Louise Abbott, Neil Mason and Zöe Stone
Designers: Claire Dale, Paul Reid and Clare
   Thorpe
Studio photography: Ian O'Leary, Gemma
   Reynolds and William Lingwood
Stylists: Belinda Altenroxel, Joss Herd and
   Helen Trent

A CIP record for this book is available from
the British Library

ISBN: 978-1-84899-201-6

10 9 8 7 6 5 4 3 2 1

Typeset in Avant Garde Gothic
Colour reproduction by Imagewrite, UK
Printed and bound in Malaysia

Publisher's Note: The alcohol rating used
in this book is intended as an approximate
indication of the alcoholic content of each
cocktail and should not be relied upon for
any legal purposes, such as the driving limit.
The cocktails in this book are intended for
the consumption of adults, in moderation.
Watkins Publishing Limited, or any other persons
who have been involved in working on this
publication, cannot accept responsibility for
any errors or omissions, inadvertent or not,
that may be found in the recipes or text, nor
for any problems that may arise as a result
of preparing one of these recipes. If you are
pregnant or breastfeeding or have any special
dietary requirements or medical conditions,
it is advisable to consult a medical professional
before following any of the recipes contained
in this book.

Follow either the imperial or the metric
measurements when making the recipes.
The measurements are not interchangeable.

Dedication:
To my family and friends, and to my beloved
readers, who appreciate the art of libations:
Life is short – fill your cup while you can.

CONTENTS

COCKTAIL
BASICS

Where does the word "cocktail" come from? What was the first cocktail and who were its first drinkers? What have been its changing fortunes? Since the dawn of time, the human race has found ways of intoxicating itself – sometimes for ritual or medicinal purposes, often for enjoyment. Drink has been at the heart of such merrymaking for thousands of years. In some respects, the cocktail represents a coming together of drinking fads and fashions from all time. From the Romans, through US Prohibition, to the present-day glitterati, cocktail-drinkers span not just decades but whole eras of history.

In this chapter we start by looking at the changing fortunes of the cocktail from its earliest beginnings to the present day. Then, we take a look at some of the practicalities of mixing cocktails at home: what drinks (other than gin, vodka and tequila) will you need to stock a bar? What garnishes should you have to hand? What cocktail-making equipment and which glasses will you need? This introductory chapter presents the answers to these questions, along with a host of other practical bartending tips and explanations to help you make all the cocktails in this book to absolute perfection.

The Story of the Cocktail

If the definition of a cocktail is a blend of two or more different drinks, then who can say when the first cocktail was mixed? Was it in ancient Egypt or ancient Rome when alcohols and spices were mixed into medicinal elixirs? Or in Aztec Mexico, where sacrificial ceremonies were performed in a haze of intoxicating spirits? We have to look forward to the 14th century to find what might be the first documented blended drink – the "bragget", a mix of mead and ale. In fact, the Middle Ages have a lot to answer for in the history of cocktails. Many of the key ingredients in the cocktails we drink today (especially many of the liqueurs) have medieval origins: apothecaries and monks used wines and spirits to preserve medicinal herbs, or to infuse the health-giving properties of herbs to make medicinal tinctures, and over time (often several hundred years) these developed into commercially produced drinks. However, it wasn't until the 18th century that anything resembling a modern cocktail came into being. While Europe can lay claim to developing the sophisticated distillation and production techniques for all the major spirits used in cocktails, it is the United States that must take pride in the creation and export of the cocktail phenomenon itself.

The word "cocktail" first appears in a US dictionary in 1803. Here it is defined as "a mixed drink of a spirit, bitters and sugar". However, debate rages over the word's origin. Some say that in the wild days of riverboat gambling on the mighty Mississippi, big winners were invited to wear a red cock's feather in their caps and to mix a drink using every spirit behind the bar. This would be drunk in a glass shaped like a cockerel and stirred with a spoon resembling its tail. Others claim that, in the days following the American Revolution, a feisty innkeeper by the name of Betsy Flanagan served meals of roast chicken to American and French soldiers. The birds for the roast were stolen from a pro-British neighbour and not a bit of them went to waste. After supper, Betsy entertained her guests with drinks at the bar – she decorated each drink with a tail feather from the unlucky fowls. "Vive le cock tail!" called the French.

However, perhaps the two most plausible of the many stories about the word cocktail are also rather less colourful. French Creole Antoine Peychaud opened his apothecary in old New Orleans in the 1790s. To measure out the spirits for his medicines, he used an eggcup – a *coquetier* in French. Alternatively, and probably most likely of all, our word cocktail is derived from the French word *coquetel*, the name given to a certain mix of wines (the actual recipe is lost to history). It is possible that Major General Lafayette, a French nobleman who helped fight against the British during the American Revolution, brought the word with him to America when he arrived in Philadelphia in July 1777.

In whatever way, "cocktail" came to be in the American dictionary, and with new refrigeration techniques, the commercial sale of ice and waves of immigrants all bringing their own ideas, 19th-century America saw the birth of many cocktails we now regard as true classics. The early 1900s were a time of great experimentation, and the hotel bars of the rich and famous (the Waldorf-Astoria being one) became cocktail playgrounds, with new creations emerging almost daily. The craze for cocktail bars quickly spread to Europe and in 1911 Harry's New York Bar was opened in Paris by US bartender Harry MacElhone (Harry's Bar was later to become the birthplace of such classics as the Bloody Mary). Even Prohibition, which hit the US in 1920, could not quench the thirst for cocktails – in fact, it ended the exclusivity of cocktail-drinking and brought it to the masses. Prohibition outlawed the production and sale of all alcohol in the US and its laws were not fully repealed until 1933. During this time alcohol consumption went "underground" into illicit bars, known as "speakeasies". Here, the bartenders had to be creative in order to mask the flavour of poor, bootleg liquor. As a result, different drinks were mixed together and served up as new and intriguing concoctions in themselves (fruit juices became common ingredients in cocktails to hide the taste of rough alcohol). Meanwhile, in Europe, a continent recovering from the rigours of World War I, people leapt at the sense of freedom and glamour given by sipping delicious drinks in fancy glasses. The cocktail golden age of the '20s, '30s and '40s was born.

If this was the golden age of cocktails then it was also a time when some of the most famous people in the world made us realize just how fashionable it was to be photographed with a cocktail in hand. Cocktails began popping up in literature and film. Famous faces were linked with famous bars throughout Europe and the Americas. Ernest Hemingway was perhaps the era's most prolific celebrity cocktail-drinker. A regular at Harry's Bar in both Paris and Venice, the Bloody Mary is said to have been invented especially to cure his hangovers.

Despite Hemingway's most valiant efforts, after World War II there was a general dip in cocktail consumption throughout the world, but especially in Europe (some say that 1950s America was a period of "atomic" cocktails – drinking buoyed up by post-war optimism). By the 1960s, in Europe and the US, when "free love" and more altered-state forms of intoxication were popular, the meagre cocktail was nowhere to be seen. It wasn't until the 1980s that things looked up again for cocktails. With fresh ad campaigns for drinks brands and the launch of new brands such as (more recently) Absolut, came renewed interest in mixing drinks. Now we can enjoy cocktails in cocktail bars old and new in every town and city in the world. Try the Rainbow Room in New York (at sunset on a clear day is best); watch the rich and famous go by at the Sanderson in London; imagine yourself sat next to Hemingway himself at Harry's Bar in Venice (arrive by gondola – it's the best way) – and if you are there during the Venice Film Festival, expect to rub shoulders with the A-list movie stars of the day. No matter what its changing fortunes in the past, the cocktail is a feel-good drink and always has been. With spirits and liqueurs getting ever more sophisticated, we might think that the story of the cocktail has really only just begun.

How to Use This Book

The purpose of this book is to give you an array of traditional and contemporary gin-, vodka- and tequila-based cocktails with which to experiment and enjoy. Some have been chosen because they are classics in the cocktail world. The most important of these are given special feature pages in the relevant chapter of the book. Each of them is labelled to identify whether it is a traditional (created earlier than 1960) or a modern classic, and each is given a short history so that you can find out why it deserves its status. However, there are many other cocktails in the book that you will have heard of – including such famous blends as the Singapore Sling and the Cosmopolitan, so be sure to flick through the whole collection. All of the mixes have been selected (from my personal database of more than 4,000 cocktails) to give you a range of ideas to both delight and challenge your palate, as well as enthrall your guests. Each recipe serves one person, unless otherwise specified.

The book is divided up into chapters according to "base" ingredient – the ingredient in the cocktail that will most influence the flavour. All of the cocktails are numbered (cross-references between cocktails refer to the cocktail numbers, not page numbers). A suggested glass type is given for every cocktail (see pp.26–27 for detailed information about glasses), and each mix has an alcohol rating in a series of filled or part-filled circles (◐◑◕●), representing one-quarter, one half, three-quarters and one whole. One filled circle is roughly equivalent to one unit of alcohol. However, the alcohol ratings have been adjusted to allow for certain effects that mixing and preparing the cocktails might have on the alcoholic nature of the drink.

For example, a vigorously shaken cocktail marginally loses some of its alcoholic content, while cocktails with several different spirits (especially if they are different colours) can have a more alcoholic effect on the body than their "unit" quantities might suggest. Similarly, the unit system does not account for the amount of alcohol by volume (abv) in certain spirits – adjustments have been made for very alcoholic drinks, too. The alcohol rating is intended only as a guide to alcoholic content and should not be relied upon for any legal purposes, such as the driving limit or the limit for operating heavy machinery.

Finally, at the end of the book the cocktails are listed in alphabetical order, with their recipe number alongside, so you can quickly and easily find the mix you're looking for.

How to Stock a Bar

In a well-stocked home bar it is essential to have the basic spirits and fine liqueurs, as well as a range of mixers and a variety of suitable garnishes. The following pages form a guide to the main spirits, mixers and garnishes that appear in the cocktails in this book – the more of these you can amass, the more fun you can have! Explanations are given for more unusual drinks.

Spirits and liqueurs
Having bottles of good-quality gin, vodka and tequila in your bar is essential for the the cocktails in this book. Other spirits, such as fruit brandies, are listed on the pages that follow. Liqueurs are highly sweetened, spirit-based drinks, flavoured (by a variety of techniques) with one or more (and sometimes more than a hundred) herbs, spices, fruits, flowers, barks or seeds. The following list is a glossary of some of the weird and wonderful spirits and liqueurs you might find in the perfect bar. Each entry gives a rounded "alcohol by volume" (abv) percentage. Just as you might expect, abv gives an indication of alcoholic strength of each drop of drink. A note to the uninitiated: the mixture of generic and brand names

used in the world of cocktails can be confusing. Where possible, I have stuck with generic names unless a particular brand really is what's needed for a certain cocktail. Also, under the definitions of some generic names, I have mentioned some of the common brands you may come across for ease of reference. Finally, some unique liqueurs that have been around for hundreds of years are known only by their brand names – this, too, will be indicated in the definitions.

Absinthe: *see* **Pernod**

Amaretto: An almond-flavoured liqueur, commercially produced in Italy since the late 18th century (but perhaps invented in 1525). It is made by macerating (soaking) almonds and apricot kernels (principally) in neutral spirit. (30% abv)

Bénédictine: Created in 1510, making it perhaps the world's oldest liqueur, Bénédictine is the brand name of a sweet, herbal liqueur first made by Benedictine monks in a Normandy abbey. The recipe, which has never been successfully copied, includes 27 plants and herbs. The drink takes three years to produce. (40% abv)

Bitters: A generic term, sometimes given in its Italian form *amari*, for a range of bitter-tasting alcoholic drinks made from macerating a mix of bitter flowers, roots, fruits and peels in a neutral spirit. Bitters are most commonly used in small quantities to give a cocktail a distinctive, non-sweet flavour. The well-known brand Angostura bitters (invented in Venezuela in 1824 but now produced in Jamaica; 45% abv) and orange bitters (20% abv) are the two types of bitters most frequently used in cocktails.

Campari: A bright red *amaro* (bitter), Campari was invented in the 1860s by the Milanese café-owner Gaspare Campari. This extremely dry liqueur (usually drunk as an apéritif) has a strong quinine flavour. (25% abv)

Chambord: A brand name for a distinctive French black raspberry liqueur. (25% abv)

Chartreuse: This branded liqueur has been made by Carthusian monks in southeast France since 1603 (but the recipe itself is believed to date from much earlier than this). At any one time only three monks are permitted to know the secret recipe, which contains 130 different herbs and spices. Two different varieties are available: green (invented by the monks in 1745) and yellow (1840). Green Chartreuse has the higher alcoholic content (55% abv compared with 40% for the yellow).

Cream Liqueurs and "Crème de" Liqueurs: There is a distinct difference between what we call "cream liqueurs" and those known as "crème de". A cream liqueur, such a Bailey's Irish Cream (17% abv) is a heavy, sweet, cream-based liqueur with a relatively low alcohol content owing to the high proportion of cream. "Crème de" liqueurs (20–30% abv) are rich, sweet liqueurs that are dominated by one particular flavour but do not contain cream. They are usually made by adding fruit concentrates to a base spirit, and occasionally by adding essential oils. Their names are sometimes anglicized, hence you may see "crème de banane" called simply "banana liqueur". The following types of "crème de" liqueurs can be found in my recipes: crème de cacao (cocoa and vanilla); crème de cassis (blackcurrant); crème de framboises (raspberry); crème de menthe (peppermint); and crème de mûre (blackberry). Crème de cacao can be found in both brown and white varieties and crème de menthe can be either white or green. In each case the flavour is the same – the selection of one over the other is usually to do with the look of the cocktail.

Curaçao: An orange-flavoured liqueur made by soaking the bitter peel of the curaçao orange (from the Caribbean island of the same name) and several other ingredients in a mixture of water and neutral alcohol and then re-distilling to release the fruit's essential oils. The distillation is then blended with a neutral spirit or brandy. Curaçao can be coloured for visual effect, the most popular varieties being orange and blue. (20–40% abv). *See also* **Triple Sec.**

Fortified Wines: Madeira, port and sherry, made in Madeira, Portugal and Spain respectively, are all ordinary wines fortified with another form of alcohol. In the case of Madeira (20% abv), this alcohol is something called "deaf wine" – a grape juice prevented from fermenting by the addition of brandy. Port (20% abv) is fortified simply by adding a neutral spirit during the fermentation of the grapes. Doing so prevents the grapes from completing fermentation, resulting in port's sweetness. Sherry (15–20% abv) is fortified using a neutral spirit once fermentation is complete. A basic rule for including these drinks in cocktails is to buy an expensive brand as it will definitely make for a better drink. *See also* **Vermouth**.

Frangelico: Named after the 17th-century Italian monk who created it, this is a sweet, hazelnut liqueur made by steeping hazelnuts, berries and a host of other secret ingredients in a neutral spirit. (25% abv)

Fruit Brandies: Strictly, a fruit brandy is a spirit that has been distilled directly from the fruit iself, usually from the flesh and, where relevant, stones. However, cocktail-makers these days use the term "fruit brandy" also to mean a fruit liqueur (see p.16). As a general rule apple brandies are readily available in the strictest sense. Other fruit brandies are often labelled as "fruit brandy liqueur".

True apple brandy is distilled directly from apples. Calvados (after the region in France where it is produced; 40–45% abv) is the best-known. However, calvados now has an equally good, younger US cousin, known as applejack. To avoid any confusion, the recipes in this book always list "applejack or calvados" when true apple brandy is required. "Apple brandy" refers to apple brandy liqueurs.

True cherry brandy is known as "kirsch" (or *Kirschwasser* in German; 45% abv). As with apple brandy, the recipes list kirsch when the true brandy is required. A reference to "cherry brandy" means that you can use cherry brandy liqueur.

Apricot brandy means the brandy liqueur, simply because it is easier to buy than the brandy distilled from the fruit.

Fruit Liqueurs: Any alcoholic drink in which the fruit has been infused in a base spirit. *See also* **Fruit Brandies** *and* **Schnapps**.

Galliano: An Italian branded liqueur first made in Tuscany by distiller Arturo Vaccari (who named it after a famous Italian general). Galliano is golden in colour and is a sweet blend of more than 40 herbs and fruits, all overlaid with vanilla. (40% abv)

Kahlúa: A Mexican brand of coffee-crème liqueur. Tia Maria is a good alternative. (25–30% abv)

Madeira: *see* **Fortified Wines**.

Maraschino: This clear, Italian cherry liqueur is made by macerating (steeping in a neutral spirit) the whole marasca cherry (stem, skin, flesh and stone). Marasca cherries that have been preserved in this way take the name "maraschino cherries" – often used as cocktail garnishes (see p.19). For the maraschino liqueur required in these cocktails, invest in a jar of good-quality maraschino cherries and use the syrup. (30% abv)

Midori: A Japanese brand of sweet, bright green melon liqueur. (20% abv)

Parfait Amour: The generic name for an unusual, highly perfumed liqueur. Parfait amour is based on crème de violette with a citrus orange twist. (25% abv)

Pernod: A liquorice-tasting spirit, which gained popularity in the early part of the 20th century as a substitute for the widely banned absinthe. Pernod replaced absinthe's wormwood (which is a hallucinogen in large doses) with star anise. (45% abv)

Port: *see* **Fortified Wines**.

Schnapps: Original schnapps is a high-quality grain or potato spirit (similar to vodka) originating from Scandinavia (schnapps is actually a nickname meaning "gulp!" – the drink's proper name is aquavit or akvavit), which is then re-distilled with its flavouring (most commonly caraway seeds). Today, the term "schnapps" is more often used for fruit-flavoured liqueurs. (45% abv)

Sherry: *see* **Fortified Wines**.

Sloe Gin: A red-brown liqueur made by steeping sloe berries in gin. (25–30% abv)

Southern Comfort: Created in New Orleans in the 1860s, and first commercially produced in St Louis, this popular drink is an American whiskey-based liqueur flavoured with more than 100 ingredients, but principally peach. (40% abv)

Triple Sec: Considered a type of clear curaçao (see p.14), triple sec (40% abv) is made by macerating the peel of sweet and bitter oranges in neutral spirit. The most famous brand of triple sec is Cointreau. Grand Marnier (made by macerating bitter oranges in cognac and adding sugar syrup; 40% abv) is often used as a triple sec. Although this is not strictly accurate (there are no sweet oranges in Grand Marnier and it is not clear but golden in colour because of the cognac), the distinction is rarely made in cocktail-making, and it has not been made in this book.

Vermouth: A basic dry white wine, infused with herbs and then sweetened and fortified. The word vermouth itself comes from *Wermut*, the German word for wormwood, and the drink is developed from the medieval practice of preserving medicinal herbs by steeping them in wine. A well-stocked bar should have a bottle each of dry and sweet vermouth. Dry vermouth is pale golden in colour (and usually comes from France); sweet vermouth has been sweetened with sugar and coloured with caramel. Several well-known brands of vermouth are available, of which Martini, Cinzano and Noilly Prat are perhaps the most famous. (15–20% abv)

Mixers

A number of non-alcoholic ingredients for mixing are also required to keep a well-stocked bar.

Carbonated Drinks: Soda water, lemonade, cola and ginger ale are essential.

Coconut Milk: A milky liquid from the second pressing of fresh coconut. This should not be confused with the sweet and sticky coconut cream.

Cream: Both light (single) and heavy (double) cream are used in this book.

Egg White: This is always listed as optional. If you choose to include egg white in your recipe, be aware that salmonella can be contracted by eating contaminated raw egg (the bacteria are killed off during cooking). Note that raw egg should never be given to children, the elderly or pregnant women.

Fruit Juices: Where possible, for best results use freshly squeezed juice. You will need orange, lemon, lime, cranberry, pineapple, grapefruit, passion fruit and tomato juices.

Fruit Purées: These are commercially available, but you can create your own fruit purées by chopping and blending the fruit with some sugar in a kitchen blender (if you make in bulk, purée can be frozen).

Sour Mix: A blend of lemon and lime juice and sugar used as a cocktail flavouring. The mix can be bought, but I prefer to make my own. Combine 14 ml (1/2 oz) of lemon juice and 14ml (1/2 oz) of lime juice with a dash of sugar syrup (see below).

Sugar: Make sure you have a good stock of superfine (caster) sugar. Brown and white granulated sugar is also required for some of the recipes.

Sugar Syrup: Sometimes called "simple syrup" or "gomme", sugar syrup is used as a sweetener. You can buy sugar syrup, but it's easy to make yourself. Combine equal parts sugar and water in a pan and bring to the boil. Simmer and stir, adding more sugar until the mix is viscous. Cool and store in an airtight jar in the refrigerator.

Syrups and Cordials: Sugar syrup, grenadine (a pomegranate-flavoured syrup), lychee syrup (taken from a tin of lychees), orgeat syrup (almond-flavoured), raspberry syrup, papaya syrup, passion-fruit syrup and lime cordial are all essential.

Vanilla Extract: A flavour made from vanilla beans. Make sure you use "pure" or "natural" (not artificial) vanilla extract.

Garnishes

Fashions come and go but there are a few basic garnishes you will need (remember that garnishes are often used to flavour a drink as well as to decorate it). In addition to those listed below, keep to hand some fresh mint, nutmeg, cocoa powder, cinnamon and crushed nuts.

Celery Sticks: Preferably left with their leaves on, celery sticks are placed in a drink (usually bitter or refreshing drinks) and can be used like a stirrer.

Cinnamon Sticks: These delicate and fragrant sticks are placed inside the glass.

Citrus Fruits: Orange, lemon and lime can be cut variously to provide a range of garnishing effects. A wedge is an eighth segment of the fruit; a wheel is a whole slice of the fruit; a slice is half a wheel; a peel is a short piece of the peel or skin (a circular piece is best), gently curled in the middle (see Vodka Martini; no.75); and a twist is a thin slice of peel, twisted into a fine corkscrew shape (see Vodka Gimlet; no.96).

Cocktail Onions: These are silverskin (small, white) onions, which come pickled in a jar. They are usually served by placing them loose in a drink or on a cocktail stick. Rinse before using unless otherwise stated in the recipe.

Cherries: Maraschino cherries are marasca cherries preserved in a jar of maraschino liqueur. They are usually dropped loose into the glass. When you are asked to garnish with a cherry, you need a maraschino cherry. Fresh cherries are sometimes used, too.

Cucumber: Cucumber sticks make great garnishes in refreshing cocktails. Simply cut a strip of cucumber, leaving the skin on for flavour, and place it in the glass.

Olives: These should be of the Queen Green variety. They can be placed loose in a drink, or on a cocktail stick. Rinse before using unless otherwise specified.

Other Fruits: Fruits such as bananas, peaches, pineapples, raspberries, strawberries and watermelon are often used to decorate cocktails. Follow the garnish suggestions I have included in each recipe – or go crazy and create some of your own.

Essential Equipment

There are some things that the mixologist just cannot do without – among them, the cocktail shaker, a corkscrew and a muddler. Here are just some of the most essential pieces of equipment you will need to make the cocktails in this book.

General

Let's start with the things you probably already have in your kitchen. A good "waiter's friend" is essential. This is a type of multi-vessel-opening device which has a flip-down corkscrew in the middle and a bottle opener on one end. A razor-sharp paring knife and chopping board are crucial for making your garnishes just as you want them, while a citrus squeezer will be useful for making sour mix (see p.18) and for small quantities of citrus juice used in the cocktails. A proper juicer will be really useful for making large quantities of fresh juices. You will certainly need a blender. An all-purpose kitchen blender will do, but be sure to crush ice cubes in a bag using a rolling pin before putting them in the blender (big lumps of ice can damage the motor) – better still, invest in a proper ice-crusher. You probably already have ice tongs (for picking up ice cubes) – an ice scoop will be useful too for scooping up spoonfuls of crushed ice. A set of standard measuring spoons will almost certainly come in useful, although for a truly professional touch, treat yourself to a set of shot measures. The basic rule for measuring out alcohol is to use the same system (equipment) for every ingredient – even if it is your general kitchen measuring jug – that way the proportions will always be equivalent. Finally, if you don't already have a lemon zester, consider buying one – it will be useful for peeling fine layers of zest from citrus fruits.

For Shaking

The most important piece of equipment of all is the cocktail shaker. There are actually two types of shaker in common use today. The first, and easiest to use, is the standard three-piece shaker which is made of stainless steel and consists of three separate parts: a tapered beaker, a close-fitting lid with a built-in strainer and a cap. The cocktail ingredients are simply placed in the beaker (when a method instructs to "shake with ice" the beaker should be two-thirds filled with ice), the strainer and the cap are fixed on and the mixture is shaken. If you are pouring the cocktail, the cap and lid are removed and the cocktail is poured into the glass. If the instructions are to "shake and strain", only the cap is removed, leaving the strainer in place while the drink is poured out. The other shaker available is the Boston Shaker, which has two pieces comprising a stainless steel beaker and a glass beaker which fit together snugly, enabling the contents to be shaken between them. An assertive tap on the side of the steel beaker is required to loosen the glass, then, if the drink is to be strained, you will need a separate coil-rimmed strainer which fixes to the steel beaker (you should probably invest in a strainer of this sort anyway).

For Stirring

Of course, not all cocktails are shaken. Stirred cocktails are usually made in a mixing glass. Available in a range of sizes, these are simply sturdy glasses with a lip in which one or more servings can be mixed before being poured or strained into a glass. Some people stir in a cocktail jug – this has the added benefit of holding several servings at once. Find one with a good pouring lip (which can hold back ice cubes). If you don't want to invest in a jug or a glass just yet, you can use the base of your cocktail shaker, just be careful to hold back the ice if you need to.

To stir, the dedicated bar spoon – a flattish spoon, a little larger than a teaspoon in measure – is best. The long handle is essential for reaching to the bottom of the drink and, as the handles of most bar spoons are twisted with a flat disk at the end, they can be used for layering ingredients (see p.24) and muddling (see below), too.

Muddling

Resembling a mini-baseball bat, a muddler has a bulbous end and is similar to a pestle. The tool is used to mash or crush any non-liquid ingredients (such as fruit, sugar cubes or herbs) before shaking or stirring. However, if you don't want to buy a muddler, a small wooden rolling pin will suffice. Muddling can be done in the beaker part of the shaker (or in a mixing glass if you have one).

Essential Techniques

Here are some of the most important techniques used in cocktail making:

Chilling, Frosting and Warming a Glass

Cocktails should be served in a chilled glass unless otherwise specified. The most effective way to chill a glass is to refrigerate it for an hour or two before use. Alternatively, fill the glass with ice topped up with water. Prepare your drink. When you are ready, simply empty the glass and pour in the cocktail. For cocktails that are served over ice, you can chill the glass by stirring the cocktail. However, this does change the properties of the drink – use only in emergencies! A frosted glass is basically a chilled glass that has a "frost" on the outside. The best way to achieve this effect is to put the glass in the freezer for thirty minutes or so before you use it. Hold the glass by the stem, so as not to make fingerprints in the frosting!

To warm a glass, place a bar spoon in the glass and fill the glass with hot water (the bar spoon will prevent the glass from cracking). Leave the glass for a minute or two and then discard the water and pour the cocktail into the glass. Remove the bar spoon last of all.

Shaking, Stirring and Blending

Shaking some or all of the ingredients of a cocktail involves placing the ingredients in a cocktail shaker, often with a generous scoop of ice cubes, putting on the lid and shaking vigorously for several seconds. Make sure you have a firm grip of both ends of the shaker and never shake carbonated drinks as they are likely to explode. To stir a cocktail, place the listed ingredients in a mixing glass or jug (or the uncapped base of your shaker) with a generous scoop of ice and stir with either end of a bar spoon for several seconds (aim to blend the flavours together without making the drink cloudy). Cocktails made with fizzy drinks need to be stirred just once or twice. Blend a cocktail by putting all the ingredients (including the crushed ice) into a blender and whizzing until the contents are smooth.

Straining and Pouring

Drinks should be poured (including the ice) or strained (leaving the ice behind) as soon as they are made to retain maximum freshness and to avoid any unwanted dilution before they reach the glass. Always empty and dry out a cocktail shaker or mixing glass before making a fresh drink (even if you are making the same recipe), otherwise the delicate balance of ingredients will be upset by any residual melting ice.

Infusing
Various herbs, spices and fruits can be used to infuse spirits such as gin, vodka and rum. Infusing can be a fun way of experimenting with flavours to create your own variations of the cocktails in this book. Place a small quantity of the fruit, herb or spice in a bottle of the suggested spirit, seal it and leave for a week or two (the longer the better). To speed along the process, you can warm the prepared bottle (by placing it in a pan of just-boiled water) for around 30 minutes. Then, leave the alcohol to cool and open a day or two later. You'll be surprised at just how much flavour has infused into the spirit, changing its character substantially.

Layering, Floating and Topping (pictured opposite)
Layering is the method by which two or more spirits and/or liqueurs are poured in sequence into a glass to form layers floating on top of one another. Always pour the drinks into the glass in the order given in the recipe, as this relates directly to the density of the ingredients (denser spirits first) and any variation will likely end up in a muddy mess. Pour each liquid in slowly and over the back of a spoon, or down the twisted handle and over the flat base of a bar spoon, to control the flow. Layered drinks are most commonly served in a shot glass. "Floating" is similar to layering, but this time only one ingredient floats on top of a mix of others. "Topping" (or "filling") simply means adding liquid (often soda water or lemonade) to the mix to fill the drink to the top of the glass.

Salting and Sugaring a Glass (pictured opposite)
These terms refer to the technique of coating the rim of a glass, most commonly a Martini or Margarita glass, with salt or sugar for added taste. Wet the rim of the

glass with a wedge of citrus fruit by running the juicy edge of the fruit over the rim of the glass. Then, dip the rim into a shallow saucer of granulated sugar or of salt. The rim should set almost immediately. For variation, you can also try dipping the glass rim into cocoa powder or nutmeg if you think it might suit the cocktail you are making. Some cocktails suggest using a small amount of liqueur instead of lime or lemon juice to help the sugar or salt stick (and to add an extra flavour to the cocktail during drinking). You can also try lining the rim of the glass with the fruit's peel for a subtle fruit flavour.

Twisting (pictured below)
To add a twist of something (usually lemon, orange or lime) to a drink, use a zester (see p.21) to remove a strip of the outer layer of the fruit's skin. Wind this slender strip of peel tightly around a drinking straw to create a coiled garnish to drape over the edge of the glass. A "loose twist" can be created by winding the peel loosely around the straw or around something with a larger circumference, such as the neck of a wine bottle.

Layering, floating and topping.

Salting or sugaring a glass.

A twist of citrus peel.

Cocktail Glasses

There are dozens of glasses available in which to serve cocktails, but for the purposes of this book I have chosen nine basic styles, one of which will happily provide a suitable receptacle for every single one of the cocktail recipes.

Classic versions of the nine glass styles are described below and pictured in the background. Each description also has a drawn icon. These icons are used with the recipes to indicate the appropriate glass for serving. Of course, there are many variations of each of the classic styles of glass (long stems, short stems; tapered bowls, conical bowls; and so on). These variations change with fashion and design, and many of them are pictured in the book. Generally speaking, I think that the more simple and classic the style of glass, the better the taste of the drink supped from it.

Champagne Flute: A traditional long-stemmed flute is perfect for all champagne cocktails. The tall, tapered shape of the bowl helps to retain the champagne's bubbles, while the length of the stem provides plenty of room for holding the glass without the need to touch the bowl (your hands will unnecessarily warm the drink if you do this).

Snifter: This large, round glass with a narrow neck and short stem is recognizable to many as the traditional brandy glass. It is used for drinking neat brandy and cognac and for many brandy-based cocktails. The short stem and large bowl are designed for cupping the drink in your hands to warm it.

Martini: Probably the glass most identified with cocktails (sometimes called simply a "cocktail glass"). Hold on to the stem so as not to warm the drink with your hands.

Pilsner: The tall pilsner glass, which narrows from the top to the bottom, is traditionally used to serve lager. In the cocktail world it is also used for the famous Singapore Sling (see no.55) and other similar cocktails.

Margarita: Although many bars serve the Margarita in a martini glass, the cocktail does have a dedicated glass of its own (sometimes this kind of glass is known as a coupette). The extra-wide brim is perfect for salting (see p.24).

Shot: Used for small but intense ice-free cocktails, as well as single shots of liquor, these little glasses come in endless variations – just make sure they are sturdy if you intend to slam them.

Highball: A tall, straight-sided glass with a generous capacity, the highball glass is used for long drinks (lots of room for ice). Some long cocktails should strictly be served in a collins glass. This is similar to a highball glass but slightly taller and narrower. However, the highball glass will suffice for all the long drinks in this book. It is probably the glass most commonly used in making cocktails.

Old-fashioned: A standard whiskey or bourbon glass, the old-fashioned is a tumbler (a short, sturdy glass) named after the classic cocktail first served in it. You may sometimes see it called a rocks glass as it is ideal for serving drinks (and cocktails) "on the rocks" – over ice.

Large Wine Glass: The idea of serving a cocktail in a wine glass might seem odd, but the large bowl is great for holding a lot of cocktail, while the long stem ensures that you can hold the glass without warming the drink with your hands.

THE
GIN
BASE

The earliest records of gin production originate from 17th-century Holland, where a medicinal drink known as "genever" (the Dutch word meaning juniper) was distilled from grain and flavoured with juniper berries. However, mass production of the spirit for social drinking almost certainly originates from England (and particularly London). There, Dutch-born William of Orange (who acceded to the English throne in 1689) openly encouraged the distillation of English spirits, while at the same time raising import duty on spirits from France. Frequently blamed for drunkenness on the streets of London, gin was the drink of the poor until the levying of heavy distillation taxes forced only the most refined (and expensive) versions into production.

Today, gin's distinctive taste comes from the addition of natural flavourings, usually during a second distillation in a "carterhead pot still". These flavourings, along with juniper itself, are known as the "botanicals" and can include herbs, spices and fruit such as coriander, angelica, cinnamon, caraway seeds and orange. The precise blend of flavours will depend entirely on the producer.

1

GIN SMASH

1 sugar cube (white)
4 sprigs mint
2 oz / 56 ml gin
1 oz / 28 ml soda water

Muddle the sugar together with the mint in an old-fashioned glass.
Add crushed ice and pour in the gin. Top with soda water and stir.
Drop in a cherry, if desired.

**Whatever you do please don't be tempted to substitute the
fresh mint with crème de menthe – it won't do the drink justice.**

GLASS TYPE: ⬜
ALCOHOL RATING: ●●○○○

2

POLLYANNA

3 slices orange
3 slices pineapple
2 oz / 56 ml gin
$\frac{1}{2}$ oz / 14 ml sweet vermouth
$\frac{1}{2}$ tsp grenadine

Muddle the fruit in a shaker. Add the remaining
ingredients, shake with ice and strain into the glass.

Fresh fruit pieces in a cocktail are a personal favourite –
they cut through the alcohol to add a distinct, fruity tang.
Garnish with a pineapple stick or cubes to make the
drink look extra-special.

GLASS TYPE:
ALCOHOL RATING: ●●○○○

3

4

GRAND ROYAL FIZZ

2 oz / 56 ml gin
1/2 tsp maraschino
juice of 1/2 lemon
juice of 1/2 orange
2 tsp light (single) cream
1 tsp superfine (caster) sugar
soda water

Shake all the ingredients (except for the soda water) together with ice. Strain the mix into an ice-filled glass. Fill with soda water and stir.

Take care not to overdo the cream – too much will take away the flavour of the drink.

GLASS TYPE:
ALCOHOL RATING: ●●○○○

DELMONICO

3/4 oz / 21 ml gin
1/2 oz / 14 ml brandy
1/2 oz / 14 ml dry vermouth
1/2 oz / 14 ml sweet vermouth

Stir all the ingredients together with ice in a shaker. Strain the mix into a glass. Drop in a cherry to garnish.

The juniper flavours of the gin are enhanced by the vermouth and sweetened by the brandy to form a refined apéritif, which I think tastes great with a cigar!

GLASS TYPE:
ALCOHOL RATING: ●●○○○

5

PAPAYA SLING

1½ oz / 42 ml gin
dash Angostura bitters
juice of 1 lime
1 tbsp papaya syrup
soda water

Shake all the ingredients (except for the soda water)
together with ice, and strain into a glass filled with ice.
Fill with soda water and stir. To garnish, add a
pineapple stick.

The papaya is a sweet and bitter fruit (sweetest in the
middle and more bitter toward the outside), which
gives a complementary taste when paired with gin.

GLASS TYPE: ☐
ALCOHOL RATING: ●●○○○

6

HULA-HULA

1½ oz / 42 ml gin
¾ oz / 21 ml orange juice
¼ tsp superfine (caster) sugar

Shake all of the ingredients together with ice
and strain into the glass.

For a sweeter option try this in a glass rimmed with sugar.
As you drink, work your way around the rim of the glass,
tasting the sugar before you take each sip.

GLASS TYPE: Y
ALCOHOL RATING: ●◑○○○

7

CRYSTAL SLIPPER

1 1/2 oz / 42 ml gin
1/2 oz / 14 ml blue curaçao
2 dashes orange bitters

Pour the ingredients into a shaker; shake with ice
and strain into the glass. Place an orange twist inside
the glass to garnish.

A blue, orange-flavoured
gin martini – quaint but simple.

_____

GLASS TYPE: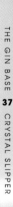
ALCOHOL RATING: ●●○○○

8

STAR DAISY

1 oz / 28 ml gin
1 oz / 28 ml applejack or calvados
juice of $^1/_2$ lemon
1 tsp grenadine
$^1/_2$ tsp superfine (caster) sugar

Shake all the ingredients with ice and strain into a glass. Add an ice cube. Put 2 slices of lemon and 2 slices of green apple, and even a cherry if desired, into the glass to garnish.

If this drink is too strong for your palate, you can dilute it with some soda water.

GLASS TYPE:
ALCOHOL RATING: ●●○○○

traditional classic

ABOUT THE

TOM COLLINS

A "collins" has become a generic term for any spirit-based cocktail made with lemon juice, sugar syrup and soda, hence the Brandy Collins, Rum Collins and Vodka Collins to name but three. However, its origins reputedly date back more than one hundred years, when the original gin-based drink, the Tom Collins, was first given its name. The story goes that a London bartender named John Collins first created the cocktail using Dutch Genever gin – a gin sweetened with sugar and glycerine, and one far more commonly available at the end of the 19th century than it is today. Genever gin was also known as "Old Tom", and so the drink created by John Collins rather confusedly became the Tom Collins. These days the two names have become almost interchangeable. However, if you are ordering the drink in a bar, always check the ingredients list or qualify which spirit base you are expecting – on some cocktail menus a John Collins is the name given to a whiskey-based drink while the Tom Collins remains its gin-based brother.

The Tom Collins is both a very popular and an incredibly classy drink. A tall, refreshing blend that masks an alcoholic kick, the cocktail seems most at home being idly enjoyed on hot summer days.

9

TOM COLLINS

2 oz / 56 ml gin
juice of ½ lemon
1 tsp superfine (caster) sugar
soda water

Shake the first 3 ingredients together with ice and strain
into an ice-filled glass. Fill with soda water and stir.
Garnish with an orange slice and a cherry.

GLASS TYPE: 🥂
ALCOHOL RATING: ●●○○○

10

GIMLET

1½ oz / 42 ml gin
1 oz / 28 ml lime cordial

Shake the ingredients together
with ice, and strain into a martini
glass. Place a tight lime twist inside
the glass to garnish. Alternatively,
pour the ingredients into an old-
fashioned glass filled with ice.
Garnish as before.

The famous gin Gimlet is thought to
have originated in the British Navy,
taking its name from the 18th-century
tool used to tap barrels. The lime cordial
balances this sharp-tasting drink, which
begins sour and finishes sweet. (See
no.96 for the Vodka Gimlet.)

GLASS TYPE: ♡ ▭
ALCOHOL RATING: ●◑○○○

11

LEAVE-IT-TO-ME

1½ oz / 42 ml gin
¼ tsp maraschino
1 tsp lemon juice
1 tsp raspberry syrup

Pour all of the ingredients into a
shaker. Stir with ice. Strain the mix
into the glass.

You can use raspberry purée instead of
raspberry syrup (see p.18) to give this
cocktail more texture. However, purée
has a more subtle flavour than syrup, and
so you may also wish to use a dash of
raspberry liqueur to enhance the taste.

GLASS TYPE: ♡
ALCOHOL RATING: ●●○○○

BLUE DEVIL

1 oz / 28 ml gin
1/2 tsp blue curaçao
1 tbsp maraschino
juice of 1 lime or 1/2 lemon

Shake the ingredients together with ice, and strain the mix
into the glass. Drop in a maraschino cherry to garnish.

**The blue curaçao makes this drink go blue but,
despite its name and appearance, the cocktail tastes of
oranges because curaçao is an orange-flavoured liqueur.**

GLASS TYPE: ⅄

ALCOHOL RATING: ●◑○○○

13

FLORADORA COOLER

2 oz / 56 ml soda water or ginger ale
juice of 1 lime
1 tbsp grenadine
½ tsp superfine (caster) sugar
2 oz / 56 ml gin

Pour 1½ oz/42 ml soda water or ginger ale, the lime
juice, the grenadine and the sugar into a highball glass.
Stir. Fill the glass with ice and pour in the gin. Fill with
the remaining soda water or ginger ale, and stir again.
Place a lime wedge inside the glass to garnish.

**If you prefer a sweeter mix, opt for the ginger ale rather than
the soda water.**

GLASS TYPE: 〇

ALCOHOL RATING: ●●〇〇〇

14

FLAMINGO

1 1/2 oz / 42 ml gin
1/2 oz / 14 ml apricot brandy
juice of 1/2 lime
1 tsp grenadine

Shake all the ingredients together
with ice and strain into a glass.
Dangle a loose lime twist over the
rim of the glass to garnish.

This is a sweet and slightly sour-tasting cocktail.

GLASS TYPE: ♈
ALCOHOL RATING: ●●○○○

15

GIN RICKEY

1½ oz / 42 ml gin
juice of ½ lime
soda water

Pour the gin and the lime juice into a glass filled
with ice. Fill with soda water. Stir. Put a lime wedge
into the drink to garnish.

Although a rickey can be made with brandy, whiskey or rum
(it must include the sourness of lime or lemon juice, and soda),
the Gin Rickey is the original drink. First made at Shoemaker's
Restaurant in Washington for a congressional lobbyist named
Joe Rickey, the cocktail dates from the late 19th century.
You may wish to add a dash of sugar syrup to sweeten.

GLASS TYPE: ⬠

ALCOHOL RATING: ●●○○○○

16

SHADY GROVE

1 1/2 oz / 42 ml gin
juice of 1/2 lemon
1 tsp superfine (caster) sugar
ginger ale

Shake all the ingredients (except for the ginger ale)
with ice. Strain the mix into an ice-filled highball glass
and top with ginger ale. To garnish, place 3 slices
of fresh ginger inside the glass.

For a non-fizzy version, use fresh ginger instead of ginger ale:
pour the first 3 ingredients into a shaker; add a stick of fresh
ginger; shake with ice and strain into a martini glass.

GLASS TYPE: ▯ ▽

ALCOHOL RATING: ●●○○○

17

WESTERN ROSE

1 oz / 28 ml gin
1/2 oz / 14 ml apricot brandy
1/2 oz / 14 ml dry vermouth
1/4 tsp lemon juice

Shake all the ingredients together with ice,
and strain into the glass.

This cocktail is not as sweet as the English Rose (see no.21)
as it has no grenadine in it. You can personalize the drink by
substituting the apricot brandy with the liqueur of your choice,
such as crème de framboises or crème de mûre.

GLASS TYPE: ⅂

ALCOHOL RATING: ●●◐○○

18

CREAM FIZZ

2 oz / 56 ml gin
juice of 1/2 lemon
1 tsp light (single) cream
1 tsp superfine (caster) sugar
soda water

Shake all the ingredients (except for the soda water) together with ice, and pour into the glass. Top with soda water. Place a mint leaf inside the glass to garnish.

Be sure to shake this one vigorously for about 30 seconds – to the point where the ice cracks. Once the mix is poured into the glass, a layer of cracked ice will form on the top of your drink.

GLASS TYPE: 🥛
ALCOHOL RATING: ●●○○○

19

GIN SANGAREE

¹/₂ tsp superfine (caster) sugar
1 tsp water
2 oz / 56 ml gin
dash soda water
¹/₂ oz / 14 ml port

Put the sugar and the water into a shaker; stir until the sugar is dissolved. Add the gin and stir. Pour into an ice-filled glass. Add the soda water. Stir. Float the port on top. Garnish with nutmeg and a cinnamon stick.

To create a more fruity flavour, try squeezing the juice from a wedge of orange into the drink, and then drop the wedge inside the glass – or, add a dash of passion fruit juice.

GLASS TYPE: ⧠
ALCOHOL RATING: ●●◐○○

20

HOKKAIDO

1¹/₂ oz / 42 ml gin
1 oz / 28 ml sake
¹/₂ oz / 14 ml triple sec

Shake the ingredients with ice and strain into the glass.

Sake is a Japanese rice "wine" (although actually it is brewed like beer, using rice, water and yeast), traditionally drunk warm in cups after a meal. For a stronger sake-tasting cocktail, try mixing the Hokkaido with vodka (instead of the gin) and a little sugar syrup.

GLASS TYPE: ▽
ALCOHOL RATING: ●●●○○

ENGLISH ROSE

1¹/₂ oz / 42 ml gin
³/₄ oz / 21 ml apricot brandy
³/₄ oz / 21 ml dry vermouth
1 tsp grenadine
¹/₄ tsp lemon juice

Shake all of the ingredients together with ice and strain into a sugar-rimmed glass. Attach 2 fresh cherries to the rim of the glass for decoration.

The exquisite pink tones of this cocktail are reminiscent of a beautiful English rose.

GLASS TYPE: 🍸
ALCOHOL RATING: ●●●○○

22

MONTE CARLO IMPERIAL HIGHBALL

2 oz / 56 ml gin
1/2 oz / 14 ml crème de menthe (white)
juice of 1/4 lemon
champagne

Shake all of the ingredients (except for the champagne)
together with ice, and pour the mix into the glass.
Fill the glass with champagne and stir.

This is one of the few highballs mixed with champagne.
Usually, champagne cocktails are served in flutes without ice, as
bartenders often view mixing champagne with ice as wasteful.

GLASS TYPE: ⬚
ALCOHOL RATING: ●●●○○

23

HUDSON BAY

1 oz / 28 ml gin
$^1/_2$ oz / 14 ml cherry brandy
1$^1/_2$ tsp 151-proof rum
1 tbsp orange juice
1$^1/_2$ tsp lime juice

Shake all the ingredients together with ice and strain into a glass.

Lost and found – I recently rediscovered this great (and rather strong!) mix. Its kick comes from the high-proof rum – more than 75% abv! In countries where this high-voltage spirit is unavailable, a golden rum could be substituted.

GLASS TYPE: ♈
ALCOHOL RATING: ●●●○○

24

GIN MARTINI

2 oz / 56 ml gin
½ oz / 14 ml dry vermouth

Pour the vermouth into an ice-filled shaker to coat the
ice with vermouth. Strain all of the vermouth away.
Pour the gin into the shaker. Stir for a few seconds
to chill the gin. Strain into a chilled glass. Garnish with
a curl or twist of lemon peel, and an olive if desired.

**Some purists argue that this is the only way to make a martini.
However, although originally made with gin, the martini
is now more commonly made with vodka (see no.75) – and
personally I prefer vodka.**

GLASS TYPE: ♟
ALCOHOL RATING: ●●◐○○

ABOUT THE

NEGRONI

The Negroni is a sharp, quite bitter-tasting drink based on the colourful Italian apéritif, Campari. The cocktail is said to have been named by a 1920s bartender, Fosco Scarelli. A local Florentine count, Conte Camillo Negroni, decided one day to modify his favourite cocktail the Americano (which is made with Campari and vermouth alone) to please his own taste for a drier drink with more bite. He was so delighted with the results that every time he went into Scarelli's bar he ordered the new mix. Quite naturally, Scarelli felt that the only name suitable for the cocktail was Negroni, after its creator.

   The drink is traditionally made with sweet vermouth, but you can try it with either sweet or dry according to your preference. Some drinkers prefer the Negroni garnished with orange instead of lemon, which gives a tang that reduces some of its bitter tones. You could even add a dash of sugar syrup to soften the drink's bite. In bars, it can be safer to state your preference for a gin-based Negroni, as it is becoming increasingly popular to make the drink with vodka instead of gin.

25

NEGRONI

³/₄ oz / 21 ml gin
³/₄ oz / 21 ml Campari
³/₄ oz / 21 ml sweet or dry vermouth
soda water (optional)

Pour the first 3 ingredients into an
old-fashioned glass filled with ice and stir.
Top with soda water, if desired. Garnish
with a slice of lemon and a lemon twist.

GLASS TYPE: 🥃
ALCOHOL RATING: ●●◑○○

26

PARISIAN

1 oz / 28 ml gin
1 oz / 28 ml dry vermouth
¹/₄ oz / 7 ml crème de cassis

Shake the ingredients together with ice,
and strain into the glass.

This is a delicious blackcurrant-flavoured cocktail.

GLASS TYPE: ♼
ALCOHOL RATING: ●●◯◯◯

27

COWBOY HOOF

2¹/₂ oz / 70 ml gin
6 mint leaves
dash sugar syrup
2 dashes orange bitters

Put all the ingredients into an ice-filled shaker and shake vigorously for at least 30 seconds. Strain through a tea strainer into the glass, and garnish with an orange twist.

You really have to shake the mint into this drink, instead of letting it sit around the edges!

GLASS TYPE: 🍸
ALCOHOL RATING: ●●●○○

28

WEMBLEY

1 1/2 oz / 42 ml gin
3/4 oz / 21 ml dry vermouth
1/2 tsp apple schnapps
1/4 tsp apricot brandy

Pour all the ingredients into a shaker;
stir with ice and strain into the glass.

I'm told that this was invented to celebrate the
UK's FA (Football Association) soccer finals,
played at Wembley stadium in London.

GLASS TYPE: Y
ALCOHOL RATING: ●●●○○

29

GIN ALOHA

1½ oz / 42 ml gin
1½ oz / 42 ml triple sec
dash orange bitters
1 tbsp pineapple juice

Shake all the ingredients together with ice, and
strain into the glass. Garnish with a pineapple leaf.

The orange bitters help to bring out the sharpness of the
pineapple in this mix of gin and juice.

GLASS TYPE: ▽

ALCOHOL RATING: ●●●○○

30

MORRO

1 oz / 28 ml gin
1/2 oz / 14 ml dark rum
1 tbsp lime juice
1 tbsp pineapple juice
1/2 tsp superfine (caster) sugar

Shake all the ingredients together with ice and strain into a sugar-rimmed old-fashioned glass filled with ice.

Leave this drink to stand for a few minutes before you start to drink it – this will help to bring out all its flavours.

GLASS TYPE: ▯
ALCOHOL RATING: ●●○○○

31

TROPICAL SPECIAL

1 1/2 oz / 42 ml gin
1/2 oz / 14 ml triple sec
2 oz / 56 ml grapefruit juice
1 oz / 28 ml lime juice
1 oz / 28 ml orange juice

Pour all the ingredients into a shaker;
shake with ice and strain the mix into an ice-filled
glass. To garnish, put 2 slices of lime, 2 slices of
orange and a cherry into the drink, and mix the
fruit in between the ice.

Triple sec is not often used in gin-based drinks. However,
in this particular mix it really helps to enhance the flavour
of the orange juice.

GLASS TYPE: ▯
ALCOHOL RATING: ●●○○○

32

CHERRY SLIPPER

1 1/2 oz / 42 ml gin
1/2 oz / 14 ml cherry brandy
1/2 oz / 14 ml Madeira
1 tsp orange juice

Shake all the ingredients together with ice
and strain into the glass. Place a twisted orange
peel inside the glass to garnish.

Madeira is a fortified wine produced on the island of Madeira,
off the coast of Morocco. Matured in heated casks, Madeira
has a distinctive caramel tang. For an orangey version of this
cocktail, use triple sec instead of the wine. Be aware that this
will increase the alcoholic content – triple sec is higher proof
than Madeira.

GLASS TYPE: 🍸
ALCOHOL RATING: ●●◐○○

traditional classic

ABOUT THE
BRONX

Believed to have been invented in 1906 by bartender Jonny Solon at the old Waldorf-Astoria bar in New York, the Bronx is said to have been named after Bronx Zoo (rather than the New York borough as we might assume). Solon believed that if you drank too many of this cocktail you would be sure to hallucinate – and perhaps you might see strange and wonderful beasts, just like those he'd seen on a trip to the zoo.

The story goes that Solon created the cocktail in response to a challenge by a Waldorf restaurant customer. The customer sent his waiter over to Solon with the claim that the bartender wasn't able to invent anything new or interesting. Incensed, Solon told the waiter that he would prove the customer wrong. Solon mixed his new drink and gave it to the waiter to taste. It is said that the waiter was so impressed that he drank the Bronx straight down – in one go. Many bartenders now claim that the Bronx is the original juice-mixed cocktail.

33

BRONX

2 oz / 56 ml gin
³/₄ oz / 21 ml dry vermouth
³/₄ oz / 21 ml sweet vermouth
1¹/₂ oz / 42 ml orange juice

Shake all of the ingredients together with ice, and strain
into an ice-filled glass. Drop in a cherry to garnish.

GLASS TYPE: ⬛
ALCOHOL RATING: ●●●○○

34

JAMAICA GLOW

1 oz / 28 ml gin
1 tbsp red wine
1 tsp Jamaica dark rum
1 tbsp orange juice

Shake all the ingredients together with ice
and strain into the glass.

I think this cocktail works best with a full-bodied, fruity Cabernet
as it complements the rum, but you can try any good red wine.

GLASS TYPE: ⅋

ALCOHOL RATING: ●●◑○○

35

PALM BEACH

1 1/2 oz / 42 ml gin
1 1/2 tsp sweet vermouth
1 1/2 tsp grapefruit juice

Shake the ingredients together with
ice and strain into the glass.

Not for the sweet-toothed – although this
mix contains sweet vermouth, it's a very
dry and bitter cocktail.

GLASS TYPE: 𝕐
ALCOHOL RATING: ●●●○○

36

TUXEDO

1 1/2 oz / 42 ml gin
1 1/2 oz / 42 ml dry vermouth
1/4 tsp Pernod
1/4 tsp maraschino
2 dashes orange bitters

Pour all of the ingredients into a
shaker; stir with ice and strain the
mix into the glass. Drop a cherry
into the glass to garnish.

This cocktail also tastes good with a
champagne top.

GLASS TYPE: 𝕐
ALCOHOL RATING: ●●●◑○

37

POLO COCKTAIL

2 oz / 56 ml gin
1 tbsp lemon juice
1 tbsp orange juice

Shake the ingredients together with ice
and strain into the glass.

This cocktail is an acquired taste – the small measures of lemon
and orange add a slight sourness to the flavour of the gin.

GLASS TYPE: ☒

ALCOHOL RATING: ●●○○○

38

IDEAL COCKTAIL

1 oz / 28 ml gin
1 oz / 28 ml dry vermouth
$\frac{1}{4}$ tsp maraschino
$\frac{1}{2}$ tsp grapefruit or lemon juice

Shake all the ingredients together with ice and strain into the glass. Drop in a cherry to garnish.

Grapefruit will give this cocktail a tangy bite, while lemon will give it a sour-tasting edge – it's your choice.

GLASS TYPE: ♈
ALCOHOL RATING: ●●○○○

39

CRIMSON COCKTAIL

2 oz / 56 ml gin
1 oz / 28 ml port (sweet)
juice of $\frac{1}{2}$ lemon
1 tsp grenadine

Shake all the ingredients together with ice and strain into an ice-filled glass. Put a mint leaf inside the glass to garnish.

The port gives this after-dinner cocktail a sweet and strongly alcoholic flavour.

GLASS TYPE:
ALCOHOL RATING: ●●●◐○

40

GIN ALEXANDER

1 oz / 28 ml gin
1 oz / 28 ml crème de cacao (white)
1 oz / 28 ml light (single) cream

Shake the ingredients together with ice
and strain into the glass. To garnish, sprinkle
nutmeg on the top of the drink.

Believe it or not, the garnish is the most flavoursome
ingredient in this mix. You may want to add a dash of
sugar syrup to sweeten.

GLASS TYPE: 🍸
ALCOHOL RATING: ●●○○○

41

CLOVER CLUB

2 oz / 56 ml gin
1 oz / 28 ml lemon juice
$\frac{1}{2}$ oz / 14 ml sugar syrup
4 raspberries
$\frac{1}{2}$ egg white (optional; see p.18)

Shake all the ingredients together
with ice and strain through a tea
strainer into the glass.

**A classic drink from a Philadelphia
supper club.**

GLASS TYPE: ♟
ALCOHOL RATING: ●●●○○

42

MARTINEZ

1 oz / 28 ml gin
1 oz / 28 ml sweet vermouth
dash maraschino
dash Angostura bitters

Pour all the ingredients into a ice-
filled shaker. Stir vigorously and
strain into a martini glass. Garnish
with a lemon twist.

**The ancestor of the Dry Martini we have
today, dating back to 1887 at least.
This mix creates a sweeter and more
complex aperitif.**

GLASS TYPE: ♟
ALCOHOL RATING: ●●●○○

43

KNOCK-OUT

¾ oz / 21 ml gin
¾ oz / 21 ml dry vermouth
½ oz / 14 ml anise-infused vodka
1 tsp crème de menthe (white)

Pour all the ingredients into a shaker; stir with ice and strain into the glass. Drop in a cherry to garnish.

To infuse your own vodka, see p.24. Alternatively, you can use the liquorice-flavoured liqueur sambuca in place of the anise-infused vodka. Beware – this cocktail definitely lives up to its name.

GLASS TYPE: ▽
ALCOHOL RATING: ●●●◐○

44

HARLEM

1½ oz / 42 ml gin
½ tsp maraschino
¾ oz / 21 ml pineapple juice

Shake the ingredients with ice and strain into the glass.
Garnish with a pineapple slice, or wedge, on the rim
of the glass.

**Using maraschino is a good way of mixing gin with fruit juices,
as the maraschino enhances the flavour of the juice.**

GLASS TYPE: ⅄
ALCOHOL RATING: ●◑○○○

45

MERRY WIDOW

1¹⁄₄ oz / 35 ml gin
1¹⁄₄ oz / 35 ml dry vermouth
¹⁄₂ tsp Bénédictine
¹⁄₂ tsp Pernod
dash orange bitters

Pour all of the ingredients into a shaker; stir with ice and strain into the glass. Place a lemon peel inside the drink to garnish.

Instead of using Pernod you can try infusing your own gin with anise (see p.24) to enhance the herb and liquorice flavours of this drink.

GLASS TYPE: ∀
ALCOHOL RATING: ●●●○○

46

ABBEY COCKTAIL

1¹⁄₂ oz / 42 ml gin
dash orange bitters
juice of ¹⁄₄ orange

Shake the ingredients with ice and strain into the glass. Put a cherry inside the glass to garnish.

This drink really needs the bitters to give it that extra orange zest.

GLASS TYPE: ∀
ALCOHOL RATING: ●○○○○

47

PARK AVENUE

1¹/₂ oz / 42 ml gin
³/₄ oz / 21 ml sweet vermouth
1 tbsp pineapple juice

Pour the ingredients into a shaker;
stir with ice and strain into the glass.

As an alternative, try shaking the ingredients together with ice –
this will give the drink a beautiful frothy head, and it won't be as
strong as the stirred version.

GLASS TYPE:
ALCOHOL RATING: ●●◌○○

modern classic

ABOUT THE

BRAMBLE

The Bramble is a truly modern classic. Not only does it capture the essence of the time and place in which it was created, but it has gone on to enjoy international fame and popularity as well. Invented in the mid-1980s by legendary British bartender Dick Bradsell at Fred's Bar in London's Soho, the Bramble is a drink that defined a generation. The cocktail helped to usher in a new, prosperous era in London which saw a resurgence in cocktail bars and cocktail-drinking, and provided inspiration in its innovative blend of new liqueurs with traditional mixing methods.

This is a fruity, heady drink that strikes the perfect balance between sweet and sour with an added blackberry tang. Variations on the Bramble can be made with almost any fruit liqueur in the place of blackberry, such as raspberry, strawberry, orange or apricot.

48

BRAMBLE

2 oz / 56 ml gin
juice of ½ lemon
½ oz / 14 ml sugar syrup
½ oz / 14 ml crème de mûre

Fill the glass with crushed ice. Pour in the first 3 ingredients. Stir. If necessary, add more crushed ice to fill the glass, and lace the drink with the crème de mûre. Garnish with 2 blackberries, and a lemon slice if desired.

GLASS TYPE: ▯
ALCOHOL RATING: ●●◌◌◌

49

BELMONT

2 oz / 56 ml gin
¾ oz / 21 ml light (single) cream
1 tsp raspberry purée

Shake the ingredients together with ice and strain into the glass.
Drop 2 fresh raspberries into the drink to garnish.

Delicious – raspberries and cream. You can use frozen purée –
however, the drink will taste fresher and much better if you
make the purée yourself (see p.18).

_____

GLASS TYPE: ∀
ALCOHOL RATING: ●●○○○

50

TYPHOON

1 oz / 28 ml gin
½ oz / 14 ml Pernod
juice of ½ lime
champagne

Shake all of the ingredients (except for the champagne) together with ice. Strain into an ice-filled glass. Top with champagne.

This is another champagne cocktail served in a highball glass (see also no.22). The Pernod can be quite overpowering and it needs the ice to defuse it.

GLASS TYPE: []
ALCOHOL RATING: ●●◑○○

51

FREE SILVER

1½ oz / 42 ml gin
½ oz / 14 ml dark rum
juice of ¼ lemon
1 tbsp milk
½ tsp superfine (caster) sugar
soda water

Shake all of the ingredients (except for the soda water) together with ice, and strain into an ice-filled glass. Top with soda water.

Have you heard of the comic superhero, the Silver Surfer? I always think of him when I mix this drink – he wouldn't be able to save the world after one of these!

GLASS TYPE: []
ALCOHOL RATING: ●●◑○○

52

JOCKEY CLUB

1¹/₂ oz / 42 ml gin
¹/₄ tsp crème de cacao (white)
dash Angostura bitters
juice of ¹/₄ lemon

Shake all the ingredients together with ice,
and strain into the glass.

Cacao and lemon may seem a surprising combination,
but they complement each other in this gin mix. The different
flavours hit the taste buds separately – first the chocolate,
then the gin, finishing with a lemon aftertaste.

GLASS TYPE: Y
ALCOHOL RATING: ●●○○○

53

ORANGE OASIS

1 1/2 oz / 42 ml gin
1/2 oz / 14 ml kirsch
4 oz / 112 ml orange juice
ginger ale

Shake the first 3 ingredients with ice
and strain into an ice-filled glass.
Top with ginger ale and stir. Garnish
with an orange slice.

This refreshing summer cocktail tastes like
fizzy orange with a hint of bitter cherry.

GLASS TYPE: 🗍
ALCOHOL RATING: ●●○○○

54

GIN SLING

2 oz / 56 ml gin
juice of **1/2 lemon**
1 tsp superfine (caster) **sugar**
soda water

Pour the gin, lemon and sugar into a glass filled with ice. Stir until the sugar has dissolved. Top with soda water. Stir again. Drop in an orange twist to garnish.

Singapore Sling? No, Gin Sling. Why? Well, it's minus the cherry brandy, which turns it into a sharper-tasting and opaque-looking drink.

GLASS TYPE: ⬚
ALCOHOL RATING: ●●◑○○

55

SINGAPORE SLING

2 oz / 56 ml gin
juice of ¹/₂ lemon
1 tsp powdered (caster) sugar
soda water
¹/₂ oz / 14 ml cherry brandy

Pour the gin, lemon and sugar into a glass filled with ice.
Stir. Add the soda water, leaving just enough room to
float the cherry brandy on top. To garnish, place a lemon
wheel inside the glass, and drop in a cherry if desired.

This cocktail was invented by Ngiam Tong Boon, a bartender
at the Long Bar in Singapore's Raffles Hotel, around 1915.
A first-rate drink, and if I were a big gin drinker this would
be the cocktail for me. The drink can be served in a pilsner
or a highball glass.

GLASS TYPE: 🍺🥃
ALCOHOL RATING: ●●◐○○

56

GINLEMON

2 oz / 56 ml gin
traditional lemonade or bitter lemon
¹/₄ lemon

Pour the gin into an ice-filled glass and top with lemonade or bitter lemon. Finish with a squeeze of lemon juice.

Any old-fashioned lemonade works well here, but for the classic Italian gin cocktail, choose San Pellegrino's Lemoncello.

GLASS TYPE:
ALCOHOL RATING: ●●◑○○

57

SONNY ROLLINS' COLLINS

1 oz / 28 ml gin
1 oz / 28 ml sloe gin
1 oz / 28 ml lemon juice
¹/₂ oz / 14 ml sugar syrup
rosé champagne
dash crème de mûre

Pour the first 4 ingredients into an ice-filled glass, top with rosé champagne, and stir. Drizzle the crème de mure on top. To garnish, add a slice of lemon and a blackberry.

Created in Ronnie Scott's Jazz Club in London in honour of the great musician, this is a wonderful fruity variant on a Tom Collins (no.9).

GLASS TYPE:
ALCOHOL RATING: ●●●◑○

58

COWBOY 45

2 mint leaves
1 oz / 28 ml gin
¹/₂ oz lemon juice
¹/₂ tsp superfine (caster) sugar
champagne

Muddle the mint leaves in a shaker. Add the gin, lemon juice and sugar. Shake with ice and strain into the glass. Top with champagne.

If you prefer your cocktail free of mint pieces, then you can strain the mix through a tea strainer.

GLASS TYPE: 🍸

ALCOHOL RATING: ●●○○○

59

HONOLULU NO. 1

1 1/2 oz / 42 ml gin
dash Angostura bitters
dash lemon juice
dash orange juice
dash pineapple juice
1/2 tsp superfine (caster) sugar

Pour all the ingredients into a shaker; shake
with ice and strain the mix into the glass.

This mix of juices and bitters creates a refreshing blend
with herbal undertones.

GLASS TYPE: 🍸
ALCOHOL RATING: ●◑○○○

60

KISS-IN-THE-DARK

¾ oz / 21 ml gin
¾ oz / 21 ml cherry brandy
¾ oz / 21 ml dry vermouth

Pour the ingredients into a shaker; stir with ice
and strain into the glass.

This subtle blend of gin and cherry creates a pleasant, dry mix.

GLASS TYPE: ᛉ
ALCOHOL RATING: ●●◗◯◯

THE
VODKA
BASE

From its humble origins in medieval eastern Europe, vodka (a Russian word meaning "little water") has become one of the world's most popular spirits. First produced in Russia and Poland as long ago as the 12th century, vodka is a neutral-tasting spirit which is traditionally made from rye, but can also be made from molasses and potato. Vodka became popular in the US and western Europe in the wake of World War II, when servicemen returned from overseas with precious bottles of the stuff.

After distillation the vodka is charcoal-filtered to remove every last trace of flavour and, apart from its fiery alcoholic kick, becomes not only tasteless, but odourless and colourless, too. This makes the spirit a mixologist's dream, as it combines effortlessly with any number of other ingredients. There are also many popular flavoured vodkas on the market, which are made by infusing regular vodka with a variety of fruits and spices, such as lemon, blackcurrant, pepper and vanilla.

61

COSMOPOLITAN

2 oz / 56 ml citrus vodka
1 oz / 28 ml triple sec
2 oz / 56 ml cranberry juice
dash lime juice

Shake all the ingredients together with ice and strain
into the glass. Garnish with a flamed ribbon of orange
peel: hold the end of the peel between thumb and
forefinger above the glass and gently heat with a lighter
flame. Ensure you direct the flame away from your
fingers, and use wax-free oranges or the peel's oil will
burn black. While heating the peel, squeeze it to release
the fruit's aromatic oils onto the surface of the drink.
Drop in the peel.

**Flaming the orange peel to release the oils of the fruit will
enhance the citrus flavour of this drink, which is a fashionable,
easy-to-drink variation on the Vodka Martini (see no.75).
Popularized in New York during the 1980s, the Cosmopolitan
was originally made with unflavoured vodka and garnished
with a lime wedge.**

GLASS TYPE: 🍸
ALCOHOL RATING: ●●●○○

62

VELVET HAMMER

1¹/₂ oz / 42 ml vodka
1 tbsp crème de cacao (white)
1 tbsp light (single) cream

Pour all of the ingredients into a shaker, shake with ice and strain into the glass. Garnish with sprinkles of cocoa powder.

Although many after-dinner drinks are made with cream, there's something to be said for making them the first drink of the evening – to line the stomach, of course.

GLASS TYPE: ♈
ALCOHOL RATING: ●●○○○

63

VELVET PEACH HAMMER

1³/₄ oz / 49 ml vodka
³/₄ oz / 21 ml peach schnapps
splash sour mix (see p.18)

Stir all the ingredients together with ice and strain into an ice-filled glass. Place a slice of peach inside the drink to garnish.

This drink also makes a great shot – add an extra 1 oz/28 ml vodka, shake, and strain into a shot glass.

GLASS TYPE: ⯐ ⯑
ALCOHOL RATING: ●●○○○

64

BLUE LAGOON

1 oz / 28 ml vodka
1 oz / 28 ml blue curaçao
lemonade

Pour the first 2 ingredients into an ice-filled glass.
Top with lemonade. Drop in a cherry to garnish.

The Blue Lagoon is believed to have been created
around 1960 at Harry's New York Bar, Paris.
Try slipping a slice of pineapple inside
the glass for extra zest.

GLASS TYPE: ▯
ALCOHOL RATING: ●●○○○

65

WATERMELON MARTINI

1 slice watermelon (large)
2 oz / 56 ml vodka
dash sugar syrup

Slice the watermelon flesh away from the rind. Discard
the pips. Muddle the flesh in a shaker. Pour the vodka
and sugar syrup into the shaker; shake all the ingredients
together with ice and strain into a glass. To garnish, place
a wedge of watermelon inside the glass.

**Made right, this refreshing drink is my personal favourite. Be sure
to strain every drop of watermelon into the glass: there should
be just enough mixture to fill the glass – no less and no more.
This mix also makes a great shot.**

GLASS TYPE: ♉🍸

ALCOHOL RATING: ●●○○○

66

BLACK RUSSIAN

1$\frac{1}{2}$ oz / 42 ml vodka
$\frac{3}{4}$ oz / 21 ml Kahlúa
cola

Pour the first 2 ingredients into a glass filled with ice.
Top with cola.

**A popular and definitive cocktail, this drink was served
originally without the cola.**

GLASS TYPE: ⬚
ALCOHOL RATING: ●●◐○○

67

LONG GRAPE

8 seedless green grapes (plus 3 for garnish)
2 oz / 56 ml blackcurrant vodka
dash sugar syrup
lemonade

Muddle the grapes in a shaker.
Pour in the vodka and the sugar.
Shake with ice and strain the mix
into an ice-filled glass. Top with
lemonade. Drop 3 grapes (halved)
into the glass to garnish.

This was one of the first cocktails to use flavoured vodka. If you
can't find blackcurrant vodka, you can use regular vodka with
a dash of blackcurrant syrup.

GLASS TYPE: 🥛
ALCOHOL RATING: ●●○○○

68

JERICHO'S BREEZE

1 oz / 28 ml vodka
³/₄ oz / 21 ml blue curaçao
2¹/₂ oz / 70 ml sour mix (see p.18)
¹/₂ oz / 14 ml lime juice
splash orange juice
dash sugar syrup
splash lemonade

Pour all of the ingredients (except for the lemonade) into a shaker; shake and strain into a glass filled with crushed ice. Top with lemonade. Place a pineapple slice and a cherry inside the glass to garnish.

The combination of non-alcoholic ingredients contained in this mix means that this cocktail tastes less alcoholic than it is.

———————————————

GLASS TYPE: 🥃
ALCOHOL RATING: ●●○○○

69

WHITE RUSSIAN

2 oz / 56 ml vodka
1 oz / 28 ml Kahlúa
milk or light (single) cream

Shake the ingredients together with ice and strain into an ice-filled glass. Use sprinkles of cocoa powder or chocolate flakes to garnish.

This is another timeless cocktail and sister drink to the Black Russian (see no.66). Try both milk and cream to give the drink a smoother taste.

———————————————

GLASS TYPE: 🥃
ALCOHOL RATING: ●●●○○

70

FRENCH MARTINI

1¹/₂ oz / 42 ml vodka
¹/₄ oz / 7 ml Chambord
1¹/₂ oz / 42 ml pineapple juice

Shake all the ingredients together with ice
and strain into the glass. To garnish, place a
pineapple leaf inside the glass.

**This cocktail was created in Harry's New York Bar, Paris.
The mix of Chambord and pineapple produces a sweet,
easy-to-drink martini.**

GLASS TYPE: Y
ALCOHOL RATING: ●●○○○

71

GID BARNETT

1 oz / 28 ml vodka
$\frac{1}{2}$ oz / 14 ml blue curaçao
$\frac{1}{2}$ oz / 14 ml parfait amour
$\frac{1}{2}$ oz / 14 ml water (cold)
dash sugar syrup

Shake all the ingredients together with ice and strain into a glass filled with crushed ice. To garnish, dangle an orange twist over the rim of the glass.

This cocktail was created by Gideon Barnett in 1998 for the patrons of Bill's Bar, Tokyo. Gideon set the trend for including $\frac{1}{2}$ oz/14 ml of water, which dilutes this mix immediately. The idea is that rather than waiting for the ice to melt to make the cocktail more palatable, drinking can commence straight away!

GLASS TYPE: ⬚
ALCOHOL RATING: ●●○○○

72

CAIPRIOSKA

5 lime wedges
3 tsp sugar (brown, granulated)
2 oz / 56 ml vodka

Muddle the lime together with
the sugar in a sugar-rimmed old-
fashioned glass. Fill the glass with
crushed ice and top with the vodka.

This fine lime drink is a version of the
Caipirinha – it's just that it's made with
vodka instead of cachaça.

GLASS TYPE: 🥃
ALCOHOL RATING: ●●○○○

73

JUNGLE JUICE

1 oz / 28 ml vodka
³/₄ oz / 21 ml rum
¹/₂ oz / 14 ml triple sec
1 oz / 28 ml cranberry juice
1 oz / 28 ml orange juice
1 oz / 28 ml pineapple juice
splash sour mix (see p.18)

Pour all the ingredients into a
glass filled with ice. Stir. Drop an
orange slice and a cherry into
the glass to garnish.

This is a diverse-tasting mix, and as
you take each sip you will taste a
little piece of each flavour.

GLASS TYPE: 🥃
ALCOHOL RATING: ●●◑○○

74

CARIBBEAN CRUISE

1 oz / 28 ml vodka
¼ oz / 7 ml coconut rum
¼ oz / 7 ml light rum
splash grenadine
4 oz / 112 ml pineapple juice

Shake all the ingredients (except for the pineapple juice) with ice and strain into an ice-filled glass. Top with pineapple juice. To garnish, place a wedge of pineapple on the rim of the glass and float a cherry on top of the ice.

Allow this drink to take you on a tropical cruise – think bright sunshine and a refreshing breeze, even if you're in a dark and crowded bar!

GLASS TYPE: ▯
ALCOHOL RATING: ●◐○○○

traditional classic

ABOUT THE

VODKA MARTINI

The original martini, which was created in the US in the late 19th century, was made with a gin base (see no.24). However, the Vodka Martini is now a classic in its own right and, in all but the most traditional and old-fashioned cocktail bars, when you order a martini you will be given a Vodka Martini.

Following the arrival of vodka in the US and western Europe in the late 1940s, the current predilection for vodka over gin can largely be attributed to the popularity of the first James Bond movie *Dr No* in 1962 – the British spy James Bond is famously partial to a Vodka Martini, "shaken, not stirred" – thus helping to bring the drink to an audience far beyond the exclusive cocktail lounges of New York, London and Paris.

However, purist Vodka Martini drinkers would never drink a shaken martini, preferring the traditional stirred version. Apart from the fact that a shaken martini is cloudy, it is also less alcoholic. Shaking the ingredients causes some of the alcohol to evaporate. Stirring merely chills the alcohol slightly. Usually, any olive used as a garnish must be rinsed so as not to pollute the drink with its brine. The exception to this is the Dirty Martini – martini ingredients mixed with a muddled olive – a popular variant of this most sophisticated of classic cocktails.

Extra Dry, Perfect and Sweet are the three most favoured variations on the traditional Dry Martini. To make a Perfect Martini or a Sweet Martini, use the same method as you would for the traditional Dry Martini (see opposite), except that you should strain away half (rather than all) of the vermouth. To make an Extra Dry Martini, pour the vermouth into a chilled glass and swill it around to line the glass with vermouth. Discard the vermouth. Pour the vodka into a shaker filled with ice and stir until chilled. Strain into the vermouth-lined glass.

VODKA MARTINI (DRY)

2 oz / 56 ml vodka
$^1/_2$ oz / 14 ml dry vermouth

Pour the vermouth into an ice-filled shaker to coat the ice with vermouth. Strain all of the vermouth away. Pour the vodka into the shaker. Stir for a few seconds to chill the vodka. Strain into a chilled glass. Garnish with a curled lemon peel, and an olive if desired. If possible, pre-chill the vodka to minimize the dilution of alcohol when stirring.

GLASS TYPE: 🍸
ALCOHOL RATING: ●●○○○

EXTRA DRY MARTINI

2 oz / 56 ml vodka
$^1/_4$ oz / 7 ml dry vermouth
Garnish with a curled lemon peel, and an olive if desired.

PERFECT MARTINI

2 oz / 56 ml vodka
$^1/_4$ oz / 7 ml dry vermouth
$^1/_4$ oz / 7 ml sweet vermouth
Garnish with a curled lemon or orange peel, and an olive if desired.

SWEET MARTINI

2 oz / 56 ml vodka
$^1/_2$ oz / 14 ml sweet vermouth
Garnish with a curled orange peel.

76

VODKA SOUR

2 oz / 56 ml vodka
2 drops Angostura bitters
juice of 1/2 lemon
1 tsp superfine (caster) sugar
1 tsp egg white (optional)

Shake all the ingredients together with ice and strain
into an ice-filled glass. To garnish, place a slice of
lemon and a cherry in the drink.

It's generally accepted that the best way to make a
sour is with egg white, but in the interest of public health
(raw egg poses the risk of salmonella poisoning), I have
listed the egg white as optional.

GLASS TYPE: ⬚

ALCOHOL RATING: ●●◑○○

77

HEADLESS HORSEMAN

2 oz / 56 ml vodka
3 dashes Angostura bitters
ginger ale

Pour the vodka and the bitters into a glass filled with ice and top with ginger ale. Place a slice of orange inside the glass to garnish.

The Angostura bitters add a herbal flavour to this refreshing drink.

GLASS TYPE:
ALCOHOL RATING: ●●○○○

78

'CISCO BAY

1½ oz / 42 ml citrus vodka
4 oz / 112 ml sour mix (see p.18)
splash cranberry juice
splash orange juice
splash lemonade

Pour the vodka, sour mix and cranberry juice into a shaker, shake with ice and strain into an ice-filled glass. Top with orange juice and lemonade. Place a slice of lemon inside the glass to garnish.

The sourness of this mix creates a fine pre-dinner drink.

GLASS TYPE:
ALCOHOL RATING: ●◑○○○

79

SINO-SOVIET SPLIT

2 oz / 56 ml vodka
1 oz / 28 ml amaretto
dash milk or light (single) cream

Pour all of the ingredients into a glass filled with ice.

Try this one with a scoop of blended vanilla ice cream instead
of the milk or cream.

GLASS TYPE: ▯
ALCOHOL RATING: ●●●○○

80

PURPLE PASSION TEA

1 passion fruit (peeled)
$^1/_4$ oz / 7 ml vodka
$^1/_4$ oz / 7 ml gin
$^1/_4$ oz / 7 ml light rum
$^1/_2$ oz / 14 ml Chambord
4 oz / 112 ml sour mix (see p.18)
$^1/_4$ oz / 7 ml lime juice
3 oz / 84 ml lemonade

Muddle the passion fruit in a shaker. Add the
remaining ingredients (except for the lemonade).
Shake with ice and pour into a glass.
Top with lemonade.

This mix is a less alcoholic version of the original
Long Island Iced Tea (see no.105)

GLASS TYPE: []
ALCOHOL RATING: ●◐○○○

81

VODKA SLING

2 oz / 56 ml vodka
juice of ½ lemon
1 tsp superfine (caster) sugar
soda water

Put the first 3 ingredients into a glass filled with ice. Stir until the sugar has dissolved. Top with soda water and stir again. Place a slice of lemon inside the glass to garnish.

Chic and simple – this is the vodka version of the Gin Sling (see no.54).

GLASS TYPE: ⧠
ALCOHOL RATING: ●●○○○

82

VODKA COLLINS

2 oz / 56 ml vodka
juice of ½ lemon
dash sugar syrup
soda water

Shake the first 3 ingredients together with ice and strain into an ice-filled glass. Fill with soda water. Place a slice of lemon inside the glass to garnish.

This cocktail derives from the gin-based Tom Collins (see no.9).

GLASS TYPE: ⧠
ALCOHOL RATING: ●●○○○

PARADISE MARTINI

2 oz / 56 ml vanilla vodka
1 oz / 28 ml strawberry purée
$^1/_2$ oz / 14 ml coconut milk
$^1/_4$ oz / 7 ml orgeat syrup
dash sugar syrup

Pour all of the ingredients into a shaker, shake with ice and strain into the glass. Place a whole strawberry on the rim of the glass to garnish.

This mix was created by Ben Pundle of the Sanderson Hotel, London. If you can't find any vanilla vodka, you can use vanilla-infused vodka (see p.24).

GLASS TYPE: 🍸
ALCOHOL RATING: ●●○○○

traditional classic

ABOUT THE

MOSCOW MULE

The origins of this long, refreshing drink, with a mule-like kick and added ginger zing, lie not in the Russian capital but a world away, in a bar on Hollywood's Sunset Strip. In the 1940s the owner of the Cock 'n' Bull saloon, who had a sideline in ginger beer production, met a visiting businessman who happened to own Smirnoff vodka. Between them they came up with a cocktail that combined the two with a dash of lime. The drink was a huge hit. Traditionally served in a copper mug, the Moscow Mule is available today ready-mixed in copper-coloured bottles. However, nothing beats the self-mixed real thing.

Although ginger beer is available in both alcoholic and non-alcoholic forms, it is the non-alcoholic variety that should be used to make the Moscow Mule, and ginger beer should not be confused with the much sweeter, also non-alcoholic, ginger ale. Inspired by this cocktail, bartenders have used the recipe to mix other base spirits with ginger beer – bourbon or dark rum have proved especially popular alternatives to the vodka base.

84

MOSCOW MULE

2 lime wedges (halved)
2 slices fresh ginger
1 tsp sugar (white, granulated)
1 1/2 oz / 42 ml vodka
ginger beer

Muddle the lime together with the ginger and the sugar in a shaker. Pour in the vodka and ginger beer. Shake with ice and strain into an ice-filled glass. Garnish with lime wedges and shredded ginger.

GLASS TYPE: ⬚
ALCOHOL RATING: ●❶○○○

85

L.A. SUNRISE

1 oz / 28 ml vodka
½ oz / 14 ml crème de banane
2 oz / 56 ml orange juice
2 oz / 56 ml pineapple juice
¼ oz / 7 ml light rum

Pour all the ingredients (except for the rum) into a glass filled with ice. Stir. Float the rum on the top. To garnish, place an orange wheel on the rim of the glass and drop a cherry into the drink.

If you like banana then this is a cocktail for you. Try blending all the ingredients together for a smoother treat.

GLASS TYPE:
ALCOHOL RATING: ●●○○○

86

GEORGIA PEACH

1½ oz / 42 ml vodka
½ oz / 14 ml peach schnapps
dash grenadine
lemonade

Pour all the ingredients (except for the
lemonade) into a glass filled with ice.
Top with lemonade. Put a slice of
peach inside the glass to garnish.

This cocktail has a deep peach taste and
it's designed to be sipped slowly.

GLASS TYPE: ▯
ALCOHOL RATING: ●●○○○

87

MADRAS

1¹/₂ oz / 42 ml vodka
4 oz / 112 ml cranberry juice
1 oz / 28 ml orange juice

Shake the ingredients together with ice and strain into an ice-filled glass. Place a lime wedge inside the glass to garnish.

This mix of cranberry and orange creates a simple and timeless cocktail.

GLASS TYPE: 〇

ALCOHOL RATING: ●◐○○○

88

BANANA EXTRAVAGANZA

1 oz / 28 ml vodka
$^1/_2$ oz / 14 ml light rum
$^1/_2$ oz / 14 ml crème de banane
1 oz / 28 ml cranberry juice
1 oz / 28 ml orange juice
1 oz / 28 ml pineapple juice

Shake all the ingredients together with ice and strain into an ice-filled glass. Place a slice of pineapple and a slice of lime inside the glass to garnish.

The mix of vodka and rum gives this banana cocktail quite a kick.

GLASS TYPE: ⬚
ALCOHOL RATING: ●●◑○○

89

140

LYCHEE MARTINI

LYCHEE MARTINI

2 oz / 56 ml vodka
3 oz / 84 ml lychee syrup
dash sugar syrup

Shake the ingredients together with ice and
strain into the glass. Garnish with 2 tinned
lychees on a 3-inch/75-mm cocktail skewer.

I first made this drink working at the Sanderson Hotel in
London – it was probably the most popular drink for our
female clients. The lychee syrup comes from a tin of lychees,
which you can buy in most supermarkets.

GLASS TYPE: 🍸
ALCOHOL RATING: ●●○○○

ENGLISH TEA

2 oz / 56 ml vodka
6 oz / 168 ml Earl Grey tea (cold)
1 oz / 28 ml lemon juice
dash sugar syrup
2 mint leaves

Shake all the ingredients together with ice. Strain the mix into an ice-filled glass. To garnish, put a lemon twist inside the glass and a sprig of mint on top of the ice.

The Earl Grey tea gives this drink a particularly delicate and fragrant flavour. However, you can use ordinary tea if you prefer.

GLASS TYPE: 🥛
ALCOHOL RATING: ●●○○○

91

MADRASKI

1 kiwi fruit (peeled)
1½ oz / 42 ml vodka
2 oz / 56 ml cranberry juice
1 oz / 28 ml orange juice

Muddle the kiwi in a shaker and pour in the vodka,
cranberry and orange. Shake all the ingredients
together with ice and strain into an ice-filled glass.
Place a peeled slice of kiwi on the rim of the glass
to garnish.

The addition of kiwi makes this cocktail a fresh-fruit version of
the Madras (see no.87).

GLASS TYPE:

ALCOHOL RATING: ●◑○○○

92

NAKED PRETZEL

¾ oz / 21 ml vodka
1 oz / 28 ml Midori
½ oz / 14 ml crème de cassis
2 oz / 56 ml pineapple juice

Pour all of the ingredients into a
glass filled with ice and stir. Put a
pineapple slice and a pineapple
leaf inside the glass to garnish.

This cocktail was invented by a bartender
friend of mine, but I've never been able to
find out the origins of its name.

GLASS TYPE: 🥃
ALCOHOL RATING: ●●◑○○

93

CAPPUCCINO COCKTAIL

¾ oz / 21 ml vodka
¾ oz / 21 ml Kahlúa
a single espresso (hot)
¾ oz / 21 ml light (single) cream
dash sugar syrup

Pour all of the ingredients into a shaker,
shake and strain into a martini glass. Use
sprinkles of cocoa powder or chocolate
flakes to garnish.

The best way to be woken up – well, almost! This cocktail
also makes a good shot, but be warned, too many may
cause a caffeine overload.

GLASS TYPE:
ALCOHOL RATING: ●●○○○

94

POLISH BREEZE

2 oz / 56 ml bison grass vodka
4 oz / 112 ml apple juice
2 oz / 56 ml cranberry juice
1/4 lime

Pour all the ingredients into a glass
filled with ice, and stir. Add a squeeze
of lime and a straw.

Bison grass vodka, or Zubrowka, is a
fragrant Polish vodka flavoured with grass
from plains where the wild bison roam.

GLASS TYPE: 🍹
ALCOHOL RATING: ●●◐○○

95

BAY BREEZE

2 oz / 56 ml vodka
4 oz / 112 ml pineapple juice
2 oz / 56 ml cranberry juice

Pour all of the ingredients into a glass
filled with ice, and stir. Add a straw
and a stick of pineapple to garnish.

A sweeter Sea Breeze (see no.101), with a
touch of the tropics.

GLASS TYPE: 🍹
ALCOHOL RATING: ●●◐○○

96

VODKA GIMLET

1½ oz / 42 ml vodka
1 oz / 28 ml lime cordial
1 tsp superfine (caster) sugar (optional)

Shake all the ingredients together with ice and strain
into a martini glass. Garnish with a tight lime twist.
Alternatively, you can serve the Gimlet on the rocks in an
old-fashioned glass: fill the glass with ice and, as before,
shake with ice and strain the mix into the glass

**This is the vodka version of the
gin-based Gimlet (see no.10).
I love the crunch of sugar
served over ice – but you
can use sugar syrup if you
prefer a smoother texture.**

see no.10

GLASS TYPE: ⅞ 🍸
ALCOHOL RATING: ●●○○○

97

VODKA GRASSHOPPER

¾ oz / 21 ml vodka
¾ oz / 21 ml crème de cacao (white)
¾ oz / 21 ml crème de menthe (green)

Shake the ingredients together with ice and strain
into a glass filled with crushed ice. Put a sprig of
mint inside the glass to garnish.

I'm not a lover of crème de menthe – but if you are,
you'll enjoy this one.

GLASS TYPE: ⬚

ALCOHOL RATING: ●●◑○○

98

HARVEY WALLBANGER

1 oz / 28 ml vodka
4 oz / 112 ml orange juice
½ oz / 14 ml Galliano

Pour the vodka and the orange juice into
a glass filled with ice. Stir. Float the Galliano
on top. Place a slice of orange inside the
glass to garnish.

The popular story behind the name of this drink is that a '60s
Manhattan surfer, named Harvey, used to celebrate surfing wins
with his signature mix of vodka, orange juice and Galliano. One
victorious day he began to bang his surfboard against the walls
of the bar, and this renowned cocktail was named.

GLASS TYPE: ⬚
ALCOHOL RATING: ●●○○○○

traditional classic

ABOUT THE

BLOODY MARY

Acclaimed by many as a good hangover cure, this distinctive classic cocktail is thought to have been created at Harry's New York Bar in Paris in the 1920s and is popularly believed to have been named after Queen Mary Tudor of England, whose ruthless persecution of Protestants during her short reign (1553–1558) earned her the nickname "Bloody Mary".

The Bloody Mary tended originally to be presented in a themed glass in the shape of a cockerel or a boat, but in today's bars the drink is usually served in a highball glass. There is much passionate debate among bartenders as to what constitutes the perfect Bloody Mary. Of all the classic cocktails, this cocktail can be most easily tailored to the individual drinker's specific tastes and there are many variations. Increasingly, up-market bars like to create their own gourmet tomato pastes to add to their own fresh tomato juice. These pastes may be mixed with myriad different herbs, such as rosemary and basil. Some better-known variations of the Bloody Mary include the addition of clam juice or beef extract to the mix. Experiment to create your own personal classic by adding or subtracting any number of the Bloody Mary's secondary ingredients (the vodka and tomato juice are essential): add some avocado for a Mexican flavour, or try Japanese wasabi instead of horseradish for a hint of the East – the possibilities are endless!

99

BLOODY MARY

1 1/2 oz / 42 ml vodka
4 oz / 112 ml tomato juice
1/2 tsp horseradish
1/2 tsp Worcestershire sauce
2 or 3 drops Tabasco sauce
dash lemon juice
salt and pepper to taste

Shake all the ingredients together with ice and strain into
an ice-filled glass. Garnish with a slice of lemon or lime,
a stick of celery and cracked black pepper.

GLASS TYPE: ⏁
ALCOHOL RATING: ●❶○○○○

100

BLOODY MARY NO. 2

1¹/₂ oz / 42 ml vodka

dash red wine

4 oz / 112 ml tomato juice

¹/₂ tsp horseradish

¹/₂ tsp Worcestershire sauce

2 or 3 drops Tabasco sauce

dash lemon juice

2 basil leaves

salt and pepper to taste

¹/₂ oz / 14 ml dry sherry

Shake all the ingredients (except for the sherry) together with ice and strain into an ice-filled glass. Float the sherry on top. Garnish with a slice of lemon, a stick of celery, 2 bay leaves, 1 cherry tomato (halved) and cracked black pepper.

Another fantastic hangover cure. But be warned – the addition of wine and sherry make this cocktail a more powerful version of the classic Bloody Mary (previous page).

GLASS TYPE: ⬜

ALCOHOL RATING: ●●●○○

101

SEA BREEZE

1½ oz / 42 ml vodka
4 oz / 112 ml cranberry juice
1 oz / 28 ml grapefruit juice

Pour 1 oz/28 ml of the vodka and all the cranberry juice into an ice-filled glass. Pour the remaining vodka and the grapefruit juice into a shaker; shake with ice and strain into the mix. Put a lime slice inside the glass to garnish.

Topping the drink with the shaken vodka and grapefruit juice will give it a lovely foamy head. This bitter mix is quick to make – it's most popular in bars with fewer cocktails on their menu.

GLASS TYPE: ▯
ALCOHOL RATING: ●◑○○○

102

CITRONELLA COOLER

1 oz / 28 ml citrus vodka
2 oz / 56 ml lemonade
1 oz / 28 ml cranberry juice
dash lime juice

Pour all the ingredients into a glass filled with ice and drop in a lime wedge to garnish.

This cocktail tastes like a soft drink with a citrus zing – to help you reach maximum chill-out on a hot summer's day.

GLASS TYPE: ▯
ALCOHOL RATING: ●○○○○

103

POLYNESIAN

1 1/2 oz / 42 ml vodka
3/4 oz / 21 ml cherry brandy
juice of 1 lime

Pour all the ingredients into a shaker;
shake and strain into a sugar-rimmed
glass. Dangle a lime twist over the rim
of the glass to garnish.

These ingredients complement each other perfectly.

GLASS TYPE: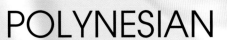
ALCOHOL RATING: ●●◐○○

BALALAIKA

2 oz / 56 ml vodka
1 oz / 28 ml triple sec
juice of 1/2 lemon
dash sugar syrup

Shake all of the ingredients together with ice, and strain
into a sugar-rimmed glass. Garnish with an orange twist.

**The balalaika is a traditional Russian musical instrument –
so use a traditional Russian vodka, like Stolichnaya.**

GLASS TYPE: 🍸
ALCOHOL RATING: ●●●○○

traditional classic

ABOUT THE

LONG ISLAND ICED TEA

Long Island Iced Tea – charming title, fearsome reputation. As its name would suggest, the drink was invented on Long Island, New York, probably during Prohibition when bartenders mixed any number and variety of bootleg spirits and coloured them with cola to make a cocktail that looked like an innocent iced tea. Today, the word "tea" is used as a generic term, meaning any long mixed drink comprising at least two clear spirits, served in a highball glass filled with ice.

This is a great popular classic – a favourite with groups of young drinkers in noisy bars gearing up for a night on the town. Beware of two things: first, that you get what you pay for. This cocktail should be an opaque, pale-brown colour. If it looks dark brown in colour, there is too much cola in it and, consequently, less alcohol. Second, the combination of five different spirits means the Long Island Iced Tea is a powerfully strong cocktail, yet it is very easy to drink – drink it too fast (or drink too many) and you will be guaranteed a huge hangover. In moderation, however, this cocktail can make a fine start to a fun evening.

LONG ISLAND ICED TEA

$^1/_2$ oz / 14 ml vodka
$^1/_2$ oz / 14 ml gin
$^1/_2$ oz / 14 ml light rum
$^1/_2$ oz / 14 ml tequila
$^1/_2$ oz / 14 ml triple sec
juice of $^1/_4$ lemon
dash cola

Shake all the ingredients (except for the cola) together
with ice and strain into an ice-filled glass. Add the cola for
colour and put a lemon wheel inside the glass to garnish.

GLASS TYPE: ⧠
ALCOHOL RATING: ●●●◐○

106

BLOODY BULL

1 oz / 28 ml vodka
2 oz / 56 ml tomato juice
¹/₂ oz / 14 ml lemon juice
2 oz / 56 ml beef bouillon (cold)

Pour the vodka, tomato juice and lemon juice into a glass filled with ice. Add the beef bouillon and stir. Garnish with a slice of lime.

From Bloody Mary to the Bull, and all you have to do is add bouillon, made up from a cube or from a can. If you're feeling adventurous, try blending all the ingredients together with a handful of cherry tomatoes and ice. Spice with salt, pepper, basil, and even a pinch of coriander if desired. Serve the mixture chilled as a soup.

GLASS TYPE: ⎕
ALCOHOL RATING: ●○○○○

107

BABAYAGA

2 tsp soft brown sugar
$1/2$ lemon, diced
6 basil leaves
$1^1/2$ oz / 42 ml vodka
$1/2$ oz / 14 ml rose liqueur

Muddle the sugar with the lemon
pieces in an old-fashioned glass.
Add crushed ice and the basil leaves,
and churn it all together. Add the
vodka and rose liqueur, stir, and top
with more crushed ice. Garnish with
a leaf of basil.

**A babayaga is a traditional witch figure
from Soviet and Eastern European folklore.**

GLASS TYPE: 🥃
ALCOHOL RATING: ●●●○○

108

LONG BEACH ICED TEA

$1/2$ oz / 14 ml vodka
$1/2$ oz / 14 ml gin
$1/2$ oz / 14 ml light rum
$1/2$ oz / 14 ml tequila
$1/2$ oz / 14 ml Kahlúa
juice of $1/2$ lime
cranberry juice

Pour all of the ingredients (except for
the cranberry juice) into a glass filled
with ice. Stir. Top with cranberry juice
so that the drink has a pretty pink
upper layer.

**This is a refreshing, fruity variation on the
regular Long Island Iced Tea (see no.105).**

GLASS TYPE: 🥃
ALCOHOL RATING: ●●●●○

WOO WOO

1 oz / 28 ml vodka
½ oz / 14 ml peach schnapps
cranberry juice

Pour the ingredients into a glass
filled with ice. Stir. Put a lime wedge
inside the glass to garnish.

**This mix is a drier alternative to a Sex on the Beach,
which traditionally has more schnapps than vodka.**

GLASS TYPE: ⬛

ALCOHOL RATING: ●◑○○○

THE
TEQUILA
BASE

Tequila, the base of America's number-one cocktail, the Margarita, is regarded as North America's first ever commercially produced spirit. The drink hails from the town of Tequila in the heart of Mexico and is made from the distilled sap of the blue agave plant which is native to the high plains of Jalisco state. Tequila, which can be clear or golden in colour, must contain a minimum of 51% agave to earn its name, and can be found to contain up to 100% agave. The higher the agave content, the better (and more expensive) the tequila.

Agave plants may have been used to make a forerunner to tequila as long ago as the 13th century. Archaeologists believe that the Aztecs brewed an agave-based drink (pulque) for ceremonial and ritual use (brutal penalties were in place for those who consumed the drink for pleasure alone!). When the 16th-century Spanish conquistadors arrived in Mexico, they brought with them distillation techniques and began distilling, rather than simply fermenting, pulque to make a drink much closer to the tequila we know today. In the 1700s Tequilan entrepreneur José Cuervo first bottled the distilled liquor for sale.

110 111

MAÑANA MAÑANA

1 slice watermelon, peeled and
  chopped
dash sugar syrup
2 oz / 56 ml tequila

Muddle the fruit with the sugar
syrup and tequila and shake with
ice. Strain into a cocktail glass
and garnish with a "sail" shape
cut from the watermelon skin.

**Watermelon melds beautifully with some
of the softer tequila flavours, and this
makes a fantastic light summer mix.**

GLASS TYPE: ⍾
ALCOHOL RATING: ●●●○○

LUCKY LILY

½ oz / 14 ml lime juice
dash honey
handful fresh pineapple, chopped
2 oz / 56 ml reposado tequila
6 grinds of black pepper

Put the first 2 ingredients in a shaker,
and stir to dissolve the honey. Add
the pineapple pieces and muddle
the fruit, then add the tequila and
pepper and shake with ice. Strain
into a glass and finish with a grind
of black pepper on the top.

**The agave plant, from which tequila
is made, is often associated with the
cactus family. In fact it has much more
in common with the humble lily – hence
the name of this tremendous drink.**

GLASS TYPE: ⍾
ALCOHOL RATING: ●●●○○

PURPLE PONCHO

1 oz / 28 ml tequila
$^1/_2$ oz / 14 ml blue curaçao
$^1/_2$ oz / 14 ml sloe gin
juice of 1 lime
dash sugar syrup

Pour all of the ingredients into a shaker; shake with
ice and strain the mix into the glass. Place a lime wheel
on the rim of the glass to decorate.

The mix of curaçao and sloe gin creates a sweet,
herbal-flavoured cocktail.

GLASS TYPE: 🍸
ALCOHOL RATING: ●●○○○

113

TEQUILA PINK

1¹/₂ oz / 42 ml tequila
1 oz / 28 ml dry vermouth
dash grenadine

Shake the ingredients together with ice,
and strain into the glass.

Although the grenadine adds sweetness to this cocktail,
it is still a strong, tequila-flavoured drink.

GLASS TYPE: ▽
ALCOHOL RATING: ●●◑○○

114

TEQUILA CANYON

1¹/₂ oz / 42 ml tequila

dash triple sec

4 oz / 112 ml cranberry juice

¹/₄ oz / 7 ml orange juice

¹/₄ oz / 7 ml pineapple juice

Pour all of the ingredients into a glass filled with ice. Stir gently. Put a lime wheel inside the glass to garnish.

The sweetness of the pineapple takes the edge off the bitter cranberry, and the whole fruit taste balances the tequila – a great summer drink.

GLASS TYPE:

ALCOHOL RATING: ●●○○○

115

SOUTH OF THE BORDER

1 oz / 28 ml tequila

³/₄ oz / 21 ml Kahlúa

juice of ¹/₂ lime

Shake all the ingredients together with ice, and strain into an ice-filled glass. Place a slice of lime inside the glass to garnish.

The lime will bring out the sourness of the tequila, while the combination of the Kahlúa and tequila will create a rich flavour to tantalize your taste buds at the end of each sip.

GLASS TYPE:

ALCOHOL RATING: ●●○○○

TEQUILA OLD-FASHIONED

strip orange peel
$^1/_2$ tsp sugar (brown)
dash Angostura bitters
$1^3/_4$ oz / 49 ml tequila
soda water

Mix the orange peel together with the sugar, bitters and a dash of tequila in an old-fashioned glass. Pour in the remaining tequila. While stirring, slowly add ice to chill the glass. Top with soda water and place a pineapple stick inside the glass to garnish.

The pineapple will release enough flavour to ensure that the drink isn't too bitter, and the water will help to temper the taste so that the mix can be drunk straight away.

GLASS TYPE: 🥃
ALCOHOL RATING: ●●○○○○

traditional classic

ABOUT THE

MARGARITA

The Margarita is thought to have first been mixed in the 1940s (although some say the 1930s), and it remains one of the most popular cocktails in the US today – in particular, for making, serving and drinking at home.

For cocktail connoisseurs the origin of the Margarita is a hotly debated subject. One of the more consistently recounted stories tells of a flamboyant Dallas socialite named Margarita Samas. Margarita hosted incredible parties and loved to entertain her guests with exotic alcoholic mixes that she herself had conjured up. Offering the mixes to anyone brave enough to try, she would ask them first to guess the contents and then to pass judgment on the taste. At Christmas in 1948, at her vacation home in Acapulco (on the Pacific coast of Mexico), Margarita hosted a poolside party for her Texan friends and family. It was at this party that she produced a mix of tequila, triple sec and lime juice. Her guests loved it and the blend soon became the society drink of the southern US, spreading quickly (from Acapulco) through Texas to Hollywood. It was named, of course, the Margarita. An alternative story is that the Spaniard Enrique Bastante Gutiérrez, who was a world-champion cocktail mixer in the 1940s, was the first to mix the drink – he is said to have done so especially for screen icon Rita Heyworth. There is also the tale of Marjorie King, a showgirl who was allegedly allergic to all alcohol except for tequila. While visiting the Rancho Del Gloria Bar on Rosarita Beach, Mexico, in 1938, she requested a mixed drink rather than a regular shot. The bartender, Danny Herrera, poured tequila over shaved ice, adding lime and triple sec. He translated Marjorie's name into Spanish, thus creating the Margarita.

117

MARGARITA

2 oz / 56 ml gold tequila
1 oz / 28 ml triple sec
juice of ½ lime

Shake all the ingredients together with ice and strain into a chilled, salt-rimmed glass. To garnish cut a thin slice of fresh lime and halve it. Place one half inside the glass and the other on the rim.

GLASS TYPE: ♟
ALCOHOL RATING: ●●●○○

118

CATALINA MARGARITA

1 ½ oz / 42 ml tequila
1 oz / 28 ml blue curaçao
1 oz / 28 ml peach schnapps
4 oz / 112 ml sour mix (see p.18)

Shake all the ingredients with ice,
and strain into a chilled margarita
glass. Garnish with a lime twist.

**The chilled glass will help to keep this slow-sipping drink cool
right to the last taste.**

GLASS TYPE: 🍸
ALCOHOL RATING: ●●●○○

119

HAIRY SUNRISE

¾ oz / 21 ml tequila
¾ oz / 21 ml vodka
½ oz / 14 ml triple sec
3 oz / 84 ml orange juice
2 or 3 dashes grenadine

Blend the first 4 ingredients together with a cup of crushed ice, until the mixture is smooth. Pour the mix into a glass. Carefully pour in the grenadine. Put a slice of lime and a sprig of mint inside the glass to garnish.

Blending the ingredients will dilute this mix. The grenadine will trickle down into the drink, giving the appearance of hair – hence this cocktail's name.

GLASS TYPE: ▯
ALCOHOL RATING: ●●○○○

120

MEXICANA

1½ oz / 42 ml tequila
1 oz / 28 ml lemon juice
1 tbsp pineapple juice
1 tsp grenadine

Shake all the ingredients together with ice, and strain into the glass. Put a lime wheel and a pineapple leaf inside the glass to garnish.

The grenadine enhances the sweetness of the pineapple. The lemon adds a hint of sourness. In essence, this is an easy-to-drink, sweet-and-sour cocktail.

GLASS TYPE: 🍸
ALCOHOL RATING: ●◐○○○

121

LA BOMBA

1$\frac{1}{2}$ oz / 42 ml gold tequila

$\frac{3}{4}$ oz / 21 ml triple sec

2 dashes apricot brandy

1$\frac{1}{2}$ oz / 42 ml orange juice

1$\frac{1}{2}$ oz / 42 ml pineapple juice

Shake all the ingredients together with ice and pour into a sugar-rimmed glass. Place a lime wheel on the rim of the glass to decorate.

For a healthier version, try this cocktail with chopped fresh fruit instead of juice. Muddle the fruit in a shaker, then add the alcohol; shake with ice and pour the mix into the glass. Garnish as before.

GLASS TYPE: 🍸

ALCOHOL RATING: ●●◑○○

122

TIJUANA TAXI

2 oz / 56 ml gold tequila
1 oz / 28 ml blue curaçao
1 oz / 28 ml liqueur of choice
soda water

Pour the tequila, curaçao and liqueur into a glass filled with ice. Fill with soda water. Drop in a cherry to garnish.

The liqueur is needed to sweeten this otherwise strong-tasting cocktail. Personally, I like to use crème de framboises or parfait amour.

GLASS TYPE: ▯
ALCOHOL RATING: ●●●○○

123

SHADY LADY

1 oz / 28 ml tequila
1 oz / 28 ml Midori
4 oz / 112 ml grapefruit juice

Pour the ingredients into a glass filled with ice. Put a lime wheel and a cherry into the drink to garnish.

For a more fruity flavour, add a large slice of honeydew melon: muddle the chopped fruit in a shaker, then add the listed ingredients; shake and strain into an ice-filled glass.

GLASS TYPE: ▯
ALCOHOL RATING: ●●○○○

124

SILK STOCKINGS

1¹/₂ oz / 42 ml tequila
1 oz / 28 ml crème de cacao (brown)
1¹/₂ oz / 42 ml light (single) cream
dash grenadine

Shake all of the ingredients
together with ice and
strain into the glass.
To garnish, sprinkle
cinnamon on top,
or put a cinnamon
stick inside the glass.

A deliciously creamy after-dinner cocktail.

GLASS TYPE: 🍸
ALCOHOL RATING: ●●◑○○

125

BULLDOG

1 ¹/₂ oz / 42 ml tequila
1 oz / 28 ml Kahlúa

Pour the ingredients into a glass filled with ice. Stir.
Place a twist of lemon inside the glass to garnish.

Kahlúa is a sweet, coffee-flavoured liqueur, produced from
Arabica coffee beans. This cocktail was invented in the late
20th century, in Mexico – the birthplace of Kahlúa.

GLASS TYPE: 🥃
ALCOHOL RATING: ●●○○○

126

MEXICAN MADRAS

1 oz / 28 ml gold tequila
3 oz / 84 ml cranberry juice
$^1/_2$ oz / 14 ml orange juice
dash lime juice

Pour all of the ingredients into a shaker; shake together with ice and strain into a glass. Place a slice of orange inside the glass to garnish.

This is the harsher-tasting tequila version of the vodka Madras (see no.87).

GLASS TYPE: ▯
ALCOHOL RATING: ●◐○○○

127

CRUSHING HAZEL

1 oz / 28 ml tequila
dash crème de cacao (white)
dash Frangelico
dash light (single) cream

Shake all the ingredients together with ice and strain into the glass. Sprinkle with crushed hazelnuts to garnish.

Frangelico is an Italian liqueur made from herbs, berries and hazelnuts. The liqueur adds a sweet, nutty flavour to this great after-dinner cocktail.

GLASS TYPE: 🍸
ALCOHOL RATING: ●●○○○

128

TEQUINI

1¹/₂ oz / 42 ml tequila
¹/₂ oz / 14 ml dry vermouth
dash Angostura bitters (optional)

Pour the ingredients into a shaker; stir with ice and strain into the glass. To garnish, put a twist of lemon and an olive inside the drink.

This is a martini made with tequila instead of vodka or gin. If you choose to include the bitters in the mix, they will add a subtle, herbal note.

GLASS TYPE: 🍸
ALCOHOL RATING: ●●○○○

129

SLOE TEQUILA

1 oz / 28 ml tequila

$\frac{1}{2}$ oz / 14 ml sloe gin

1 tbsp lime juice

Blend the ingredients together with half a cup of crushed
ice and pour into the glass. Add 3 ice cubes. Put a twist
of cucumber peel inside the glass to garnish.

This is a wonderfully smooth and fresh-tasting combination.

GLASS TYPE: 🍸

ALCOHOL RATING: ●◑○○○○

130

TEQUILA COLLINS

2 oz / 56 ml tequila
juice of $^1/_2$ lemon
1 tsp superfine (caster) sugar
soda water

Shake all the ingredients (except for the
soda water) with ice and strain into an
ice-filled glass. Top with soda water and stir.
To garnish, put a loose twist of lemon and
a loose twist of orange inside the glass,
and drop in a cherry.

This is the tequila version of the classic
gin-based Tom Collins (see no.9). Often,
cocktails that contain fizzy drinks are not stirred.
However, this mix should be stirred to ensure
that the sugar dissolves completely.

GLASS TYPE: ▯
ALCOHOL RATING: ●●○○○

STRAWBERRY MARGARITA

3 strawberries
1 oz / 28 ml tequila
$\frac{1}{2}$ oz / 14 ml strawberry liqueur
$\frac{1}{2}$ oz / 14 ml triple sec
juice of $\frac{1}{2}$ lime

Muddle the strawberries in a shaker.
Add the remaining ingredients. Shake with
ice and strain into a sugar-rimmed glass.
Float 2 strawberry slices on top.

You can substitute the strawberry with other fresh fruit –
try raspberry, kiwi or mango. Be sure to sugar-rim the glass
to complement the sweetness of the fruit.

GLASS TYPE: Y
ALCOHOL RATING: ●●○○○

132

PURPLE GECKO

1 1/2 oz / 42 ml tequila
1/2 oz / 14 ml blue curaçao
1 1/2 oz / 42 ml cranberry juice
1 oz / 28 ml sour mix (see p.18)
1/2 oz / 14 ml lime juice

Shake all of the ingredients together with
ice and strain into a salt-rimmed glass.
Garnish with a lime wedge.

The cranberry gives this version of a margarita a
distinctive "berry" taste.

GLASS TYPE: ♟ ♟
ALCOHOL RATING: ●●○○○

modern classic

ABOUT THE
TEQUILA SUNRISE

A hugely popular, easy-drinking modern classic, the Tequila Sunrise evokes images of palm-fringed beaches and balmy evenings in exotic locations. This is a fruity and refreshing cocktail with a powerful tequila kick that is effortlessly masked by the sweet-tasting grenadine. The grenadine is always added last so that it streaks red through the orange drink as it slowly sinks to the bottom of the glass to give the famous "sunrise" effect.

Although its image has suffered a little in recent years from a backlash against the genre of colourful and elaborately garnished fruit-cocktails, the Tequila Sunrise remains a popular classic – easy to mix and even easier to drink, it is a great introduction to the cocktail world.

133

TEQUILA SUNRISE

2 oz / 56 ml tequila
4 oz / 112 ml orange juice
³/₄ oz / 21 ml grenadine

Pour the tequila and the orange into a shaker; stir with ice and strain into a glass. Add ice cubes. Pour in the grenadine and allow it to sink down to the bottom of the drink to complete your sunrise. Garnish with a lime wheel. If desired, serve this drink with a straw, so that the grenadine will be the first flavour to hit the palate, and the stronger-tasting tequila will be disguised right to the end of the drink.

GLASS TYPE: ▯
ALCOHOL RATING: ●●○○○

134

POM-AMORE

¹/₂ pomegranate
dash sugar syrup
1¹/₂ oz / 42 ml tequila
¹/₄ oz / 7 ml parfait amour

Squeeze the pomegranate into the shaker to release the flesh. Muddle the flesh with the sugar. Add the tequila and parfait amour. Shake with ice and strain into the glass. To garnish, drop in 10 to 15 pips from the remaining half of the pomegranate, and float a pansy head on top of the drink.

This is one of my favourite cocktails that I have ever created – the ingredients mix so well. You can garnish your own drink with any edible flower that you desire.

GLASS TYPE: 🍸
ALCOHOL RATING: ●●○○○

135 136

TRAFFIC LIGHT COOLER

³/₄ oz / 21 ml Midori
1 oz / 28 ml gold tequila
splash sour mix (see p.18)
2 oz / 56 ml orange juice
¹/₂ oz / 14 ml sloe gin

To layer this drink: first pour the Midori into a pilsner glass filled with ice, then add the tequila, to create a layer of green. Pour in the sour mix. Slowly add the orange juice, pouring against the side of the glass, to create an amber layer. Carefully float the sloe gin on top for the red layer. Place a lemon wheel, a lime wheel and a cherry inside the glass to garnish.

To preserve the 3 colourful layers of this cocktail serve unstirred – but provide a swizzle stick, so that the drinker can mix at their leisure.

GLASS TYPE: 🥛
ALCOHOL RATING: ●●◐○○

PACIFIC SUNSHINE

1¹/₂ oz / 42 ml tequila
1¹/₂ oz / 42 ml blue curaçao
1¹/₂ oz / 42 ml sour mix (see p.18)
dash Angostura bitters

Stir all the ingredients together with ice and pour into a chilled, salt-rimmed glass. Put a lemon wheel inside the glass to garnish.

The bitters add a herbal flavour to this sour drink.

GLASS TYPE: 🥛
ALCOHOL RATING: ●●●○○

137

BLUE MARGARITA

1¹/₂ oz / 42 ml tequila
¹/₂ oz / 14 ml blue curaçao
1 oz / 28 ml lime juice

Shake the ingredients together with ice, and strain into a salt-rimmed glass. Place a loose orange twist inside the glass to garnish.

Alternatively, try blending the ingredients together with a cup of crushed ice. This will give the drink an opaque-blue appearance.

GLASS TYPE: 🍸
ALCOHOL RATING: ●●○○○

138

WILD THING

1½ oz / 42 ml tequila
1 oz / 28 ml cranberry juice
½ oz / 14 ml lime juice
1 oz / 28 ml soda water

Pour the first 3 ingredients
into a glass filled with ice.
Top with soda water. To garnish,
put a lime wheel inside the glass.

This smooth and refreshing cocktail goes
down really easily and quickly.

GLASS TYPE: 🥃
ALCOHOL RATING: ●●○○○

139

TEQUILA MANHATTAN

2 oz / 56 ml tequila
1 oz / 28 ml sweet vermouth
dash lime juice

Shake the ingredients with ice, and strain the mix into a glass containing 1 ice cube. Drop a cherry and a twist of orange peel into the drink to garnish.

This is a refined drink for serious tequila lovers.

GLASS TYPE: 🍸
ALCOHOL RATING: ●●●○○

140

CHAPALA

1¹/₂ oz / 42 ml tequila
1 tsp apricot brandy
1 tsp blue curaçao
dash triple sec
1 tbsp lemon juice
1 tbsp orange juice

Pour all the ingredients into a shaker; shake with ice and strain into an ice-filled glass. Put a slice of orange inside the glass to garnish.

If drunk slowly this is a refreshing cocktail, and it makes a good apéritif, too.

GLASS TYPE: ▢
ALCOHOL RATING: ●●○○○

141

TEQUILA MOCKINGBIRD

1¹/₂ oz / 42 ml tequila
³/₄ oz / 21 ml crème de menthe (green)
juice of 1 lime

Shake all the ingredients together with ice and strain into the glass.

If, like me, you aren't a fan of crème de menthe, you can use fresh mint and a dash of sugar syrup: simply muddle the mint in a shaker, then add the tequila, lime and syrup. Shake with ice and strain the mix into the glass.

GLASS TYPE: ▽
ALCOHOL RATING: ●●◐○○

142

TEQUILA SOUR

2 oz / 56 ml tequila
juice of $\frac{1}{2}$ lemon
1 tsp superfine (caster) sugar
dash egg white (optional)

Shake the ingredients with ice and strain into
the glass. Put a slice of lemon and a cherry
inside the glass to garnish.

If shaken with egg white (see p.18), this drink will have a frothy,
cappuccino-like head. The egg white will have only a slight
impact on the flavour.

GLASS TYPE: ⬚
ALCOHOL RATING: ●●○○○

143

HOT PANTS

$1^1/_2$ oz / 42 ml tequila
$^1/_2$ oz / 14 ml liqueur of choice
1 tbsp grapefruit juice
2 mint leaves
1 tsp superfine (caster) sugar

Shake all the ingredients together with ice and
pour into an ice-filled glass. Put a sprig of mint
on top of the ice to garnish.

This drink works well with any flavour of liqueur –
peach is my personal favourite.

GLASS TYPE: ▯
ALCOHOL RATING: ●●○○○

144

ROSITA

1 oz / 28 ml tequila
1 oz / 28 ml Campari
$^{1}/_{2}$ oz / 14 ml dry vermouth
$^{1}/_{2}$ oz / 14 ml sweet vermouth

Pour the ingredients into an ice-filled
glass and stir. Place a lemon twist inside
the glass to garnish.

The combination of the 3 types of vermouth makes
this cocktail an excellent apéritif.

GLASS TYPE: ⬚
ALCOHOL RATING: ●●◑○○

145 146

MEXICOLA

2 oz / 56 ml tequila
juice of $\frac{1}{2}$ lime
cola

Pour the tequila and the lime juice
into a glass filled with ice. Fill with
cola and stir. Drop in a lime
wedge to garnish.

If you are ordering this drink in a bar ask
for cola from a bottle, as the cola usually
served on tap is too sweet for this drink.
If you have no option, ask for more lime
to counterbalance the sweetness.

GLASS TYPE: 🥃
ALCOHOL RATING: ●●○○○

TEUTONIC

2 oz / 56 ml tequila
juice of 1 lime or $\frac{1}{2}$ lemon
tonic water

Pour the first 2 ingredients into
a glass filled with ice. Top with
tonic water and stir. Put a slice
of lemon and a slice of lime
inside the glass to garnish.

The juice of the lemon or lime will
temper this biting mix of tequila and
tonic, to create a refreshing cocktail.

GLASS TYPE: 🥃
ALCOHOL RATING: ●●○○○

147

PALOMA

2 oz / 56 ml tequila
grapefruit soda
¼ lime

Pour the tequila into an ice-filled glass. Top with grapefruit soda. Stir, and add a squeeze of lime.

An authentic Mexican treat. If you can't get hold of a fizzy grapefruit soft drink, use some pink grapefruit juice and a splash of soda water.

GLASS TYPE: □
ALCOHOL RATING: ●●●○○

148

EL DIABLO

2 oz / 56 ml reposado tequila
¹/₂ oz / 14 ml fresh lime juice
3 oz / 84 ml ginger ale
dash crème de cassis

Pour the tequila, lime juice and ginger ale into an ice-filled glass. Stir, garnish with a slice of lime and a blackberry, then finish with a drizzle of cassis.

A much-misunderstood drink from 1940s California, this is one of the first-ever tequila cocktails. Reposado is a category of tequila that has been aged for between 2 months and a year.

GLASS TYPE: □
ALCOHOL RATING: ●●●○○

149

CACTUS BERRY

1¼ oz / 35 ml tequila
1¼ oz / 35 ml red wine
1 oz / 28 ml triple sec
6½ oz / 182 ml sour mix (see p.18)
dash lime juice

Shake all of the ingredients with ice and pour into
a salt-rimmed glass.

This is a good party cocktail.
The red wine turns this drink into a
sangria-tasting margarita. I find that
oaky-flavoured wines work well with
tequila. You may wish to add a splash
of soda water to temper the alcohol.

GLASS TYPE: 🍸
ALCOHOL RATING: ●●●○○

150

SANTA CLEMENTINA

2 oz / 56 ml reposado tequila
$^1/_2$ oz / 14 ml lime juice
dash passion fruit syrup
3 oz / 84 ml bitter lemon
2 oz / 56 ml fresh orange juice

Pour the first 4 ingredients over cubed ice, then stir as
you top with orange juice.

"Oranges and Lemons, say the bells of St Clements" – the
church may be in London, but if the drink tastes this good, well...

GLASS TYPE: ⬜

ALCOHOL RATING: ●●◐○○

Cocktail Finder

Numbers here refer to the recipe number, not the page number.